Sch

LIFE

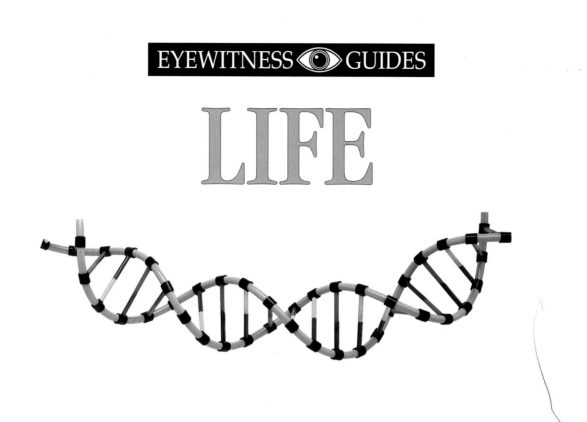

Ocellated lizard basking in the Sun to warm its body

Model of
methane
molecule

Slow-worm

Vegetable oil

Plant using up carbon
dioxide in bell jar and
giving out oxygen

Meerkats on
the look-out

Cast of internal
structure of
human liver

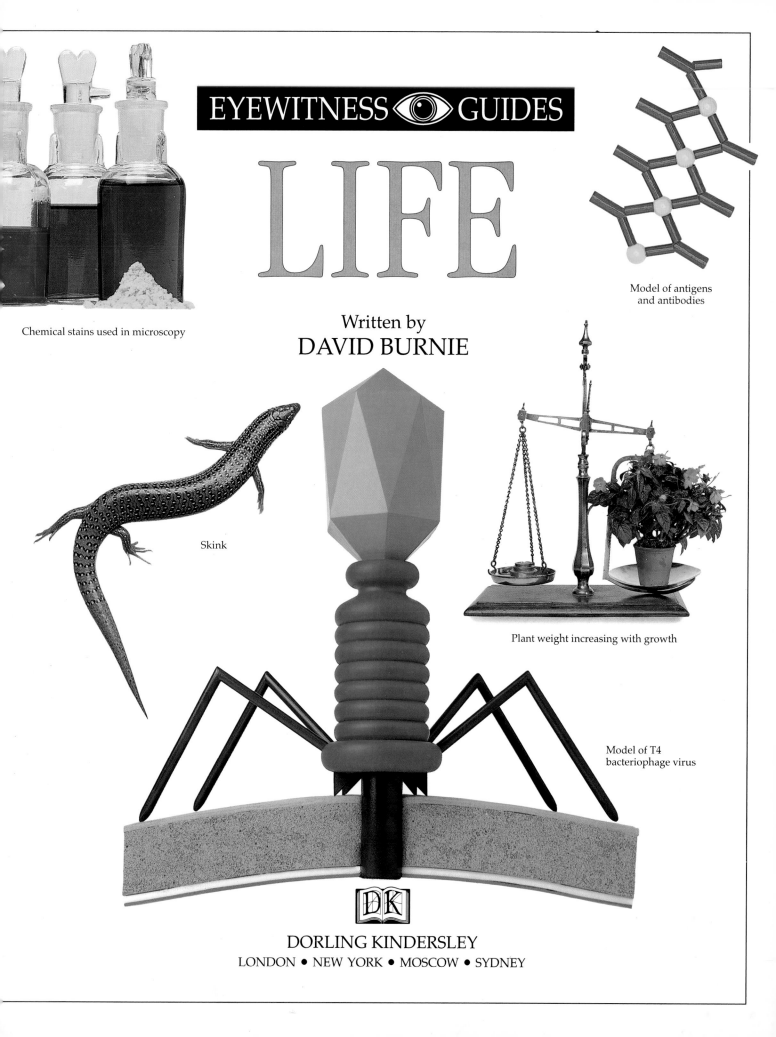

EYEWITNESS GUIDES

LIFE

Chemical stains used in microscopy

Model of antigens and antibodies

Written by
DAVID BURNIE

Skink

Plant weight increasing with growth

Model of T4
bacteriophage virus

DK

DORLING KINDERSLEY

LONDON • NEW YORK • MOSCOW • SYDNEY

A DORLING KINDERSLEY BOOK
www.dk.com

NOTE TO PARENTS AND TEACHERS

The **Eyewitness Guides** series encourages children to observe and question the world around them. It will help families to answer their questions about why and how things work – from daily occurrences in the home to the mysteries of space. By regularly "looking things up" in these books, parents can promote reading for information every day.

At school, these books are a valuable resource. Teachers will find them especially useful for topic work in many subjects and can use the experiments and demonstrations in the books as inspiration for classroom activities and projects. **Eyewitness Guides** titles are also ideal reference books, providing a wealth of information about all areas of science within the curriculum.

Indian maize

Caterpillars set off in search of new sources of food

Model of antigens and antibodies

Foxglove plant in flower

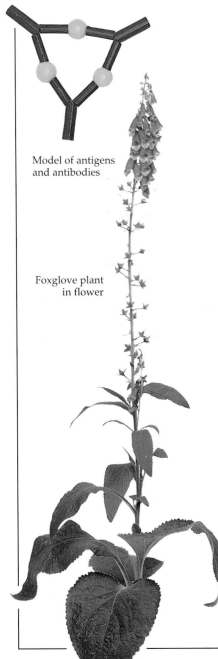

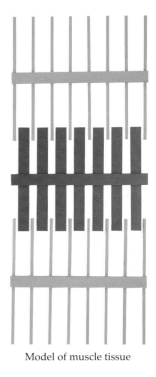

Model of muscle tissue

Project Editor Ian Whitelaw
Art Editor Rachel Gibson
Design Assistant Helen Diplock
Production Adrian Gathercole
Picture Research Diana Morris
Managing Editor Josephine Buchanan
Managing Art Editor Lynne Brown
Natural History Photography Neil Fletcher
Electron Microscopy Dr Julian Thorpe,
University of Sussex
Microphotography M. I. Walker
Editorial Consultant Dr Robert Whittle,
University of Sussex

This Eyewitness ®/™ Science book
first published in Great Britain in 1994 by
Dorling Kindersley Limited, 9 Henrietta Street,
London WC2E 8PS

2 4 6 8 10 9 7 5 3

Copyright © 1994
Dorling Kindersley Limited, London

A CIP catalogue record for this book is available
from the British Library

ISBN 0 7513 6139 9

Reproduced by Colourscan, Singapore
Printed in China by Toppan Printing Co., (Shenzhen) Ltd

Juvenile badger

Contents

Adult tawny owl with young

What is life?

OUR PLANET TEEMS WITH LIFE. Living things can be found in the depths of the sea, far beyond the reach of daylight, and also on the windswept slopes of the highest mountains. Some forms of life thrive in sticky volcanic mud that is far too hot to touch, while others live on bare rock, or deep inside banks of snow. However, despite being abundant almost everywhere, life is surprisingly difficult to define. Biologists sum up life as a range of particular characteristics that all living things share. These characteristics include the ability to use energy, the ability to take in raw materials, and the ability to get rid of waste. They also include responding to the outside world – often by moving or changing shape – and, most important of all, being able to reproduce. With reproduction comes a characteristic that is shown not by living things as individuals, but by life as a whole. This is the ability to change slowly, or "evolve", as time passes. This book explores these characteristics, and the physical and chemical ways in which living things achieve them. It looks at the very different forms that make up the living world, and travels on a path that leads through, and finally beyond, life on Earth.

MECHANICAL LIFE
Robots seem to be alive because they can move about and respond to their surroundings, but a robot relies on humans to supply it with energy, and it cannot reproduce.

LIVING STONES
For obvious reasons, these desert plants are often called "living stones". Despite their camouflage, they are very much alive, taking in inorganic nutrients and carrying out photosynthesis (p. 16), using energy from sunlight to build these up into organic molecules. Every year, they also do something that no pebble can do – they flower and form seeds.

CRYSTALS THAT GROW
Seen under a microscope, a thin slice of a kind of rock called moss agate reveals green and black streaks that look just like moss or roots. These streaks are actually mineral crystals. Crystals can grow, and some scientists think that this ability may have played a part in the origin of life (p. 54).

Venus comb shell

MAKING ORDER
This beautiful object is the skeleton of a glass sponge. Glass sponges live on the seabed and make their skeletons from a mineral called silica, which they absorb from the water. A glass sponge skeleton can be up to 3 m (10 ft) long, and it contains thousands of tiny slivers of silica, all arranged in a very precise way. This ability to build up ordered structures is typical of living things.

Chalk

Highly ordered lattice made of silica slivers

TAKING SHAPE
Throughout the Universe, matter constantly gains "entropy", meaning that it becomes more mixed up or disorganised, and so contains less usable energy. Living things are unique because, on a purely local scale, they seem to reverse this rule.
This venus comb shell is built up out of calcium carbonate, the same mineral that is found in chalk. The shell is far more ordered than the chalk. Its owner used energy in making it, and it obtained this energy by eating food.

Skeleton of glass sponge

Building up and breaking down

A living thing is a complex collection of chemicals, most of which contain the element carbon (p. 8). Throughout every second of life, these chemicals are participating in an almost baffling array of reactions. Some reactions break down complex substances to form simpler ones, often releasing energy in the process (p. 18). Others do the reverse, and usually take in energy (p. 16). Together, these reactions make up a living thing's "metabolism". In a laboratory, many metabolic reactions take place extremely slowly, but in living things they happen thousands or even millions of times faster. This difference in rate is due to enzymes – special proteins (p. 9) that are made by living cells. Enzymes are like chemical "matchmakers", bringing other chemicals together so that they can react quickly enough to support life.

THE END OF LIFE
This 19th-century French painting shows Death tugging at the shoulder of a seated figure, to take him away from the land of the living. Paradoxically, death is essential for life. Living things evolve (p. 42) through reproduction, so death allows existing forms of life to be replaced by ones that are better suited to the world around them. If nothing had ever died, the planet would have long ago been over-run by the first life-forms that appeared.

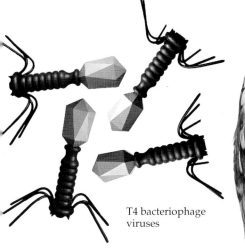

T4 bacteriophage viruses

PARTLY ALIVE
In truly living things, metabolism continues all the time. Although it often slows down – during sleep or hibernation for example – it never actually stops. However, in viruses (p. 58) things are different. A virus carries out metabolic reactions with the help of living cells. When it is outside a cell, its metabolism comes to a complete halt. This is one of the reasons why viruses are not considered to be fully alive.

LINKED WITH THE FUTURE
Watched by its attentive parent, a young tawny owl swallows a mouse. The owl's way of life, which involves using keen senses to hunt small animals after dark, is just one of a vast number of strategies that living things have evolved for sustaining life. Although living things are different from robots, some biologists do think of them as being rather like machines. Within every form of life is a set of chemical instructions (p. 34). These are handed down from one generation to the next. An owl or a tree can be seen just as a vehicle for multiplying the instructions and handing them on. Catching mice or growing leaves are just two different ways of ensuring that this happens as successfully as possible.

7

The carbon key

OVER 90 DIFFERENT CHEMICAL ELEMENTS are found naturally on Earth. Each one is made of atoms, which are the smallest particles that show an element's chemical characteristics. Of these naturally occurring elements, only about 25 seem to be essential for life. Some – such as cobalt and chromium – are needed only in very small amounts and take part in just a few chemical reactions in living things. Others are required in much larger quantities and make up the bulk of living matter. Foremost among these elements are hydrogen, oxygen, nitrogen, and, above all, carbon. Carbon is a very unusual element. It exists naturally in two pure forms, diamond and graphite, but it is much more commonly found in combination with other chemicals as a compound. In living things, carbon forms an extraordinary variety of very stable chemical compounds. The molecules of some of these have just a few atoms, while others have thousands or even millions. Only carbon atoms can link up in this stable way. Without the presence of carbon and its unusual properties, it is unlikely that there would be life on Earth.

THE CARBON CYCLE
Carbon atoms constantly cycle between the world of living things and the world of non-living matter. The carbon atoms in this piece of coal once formed part of plants. When coal is burned, its carbon is released into the atmosphere in the form of gaseous carbon dioxide. This gas is used by plants during photosynthesis (p. 16), and the carbon is often passed on to animals. In this way, the carbon cycle continues.

Methane molecule

Hydrogen atom

Carbon atom

THE FOURFOLD LINK
A single carbon atom can bond with up to four other atoms. These can be other carbon atoms, atoms of other elements, or a combination of the two. This model shows a molecule of the gas methane, one of the simplest of all carbon-containing compounds. Each methane molecule consists of a single carbon atom bonded to four hydrogen atoms. Methane is very light and forms a gas at room temperature. Larger carbon-containing molecules, such as the other examples shown here, are much heavier. They form liquids or solids at room temperature.

CARBOHYDRATES
Table sugar is made up mainly of a carbon compound called sucrose, which belongs to an important group of substances known as carbohydrates. Most living things use carbohydrates to store energy, and plants use carbohydrates to build their cell walls. Plants store energy in the form of sucrose and starch. A sucrose molecule is made up of just two rings of carbon atoms and dissolves very easily. The two rings are glucose (a hexagon) and fructose (a pentagon). Both are used in respiration (pp. 18-19). Other carbohydrates, such as starch and cellulose, have molecules with hundreds or thousands of rings, and these are much more difficult to dissolve.

Glucose ring

Sucrose molecule

Fructose ring

THE VITAL FORCE
Until the early 1800s most chemists thought that the substances in living things contained a "vital force". They called these substances "organic", and believed that they could be made only by organisms, or living things. In 1828 the German chemist Friedrich Wöhler (1800–1882) helped to undermine this idea when he made an organic compound – urea – from ammonium cyanate, an inorganic compound. Wöhler's experiment was the first of many that gradually weakened the idea of "vitalism". Chemists now know that living and non-living matter contain the same kinds of atoms and that their chemistry follows the same set of rules.

Sugar, a carbohydrate composed mainly of sucrose

MAKING THE LINK
The Scottish chemist Archibald Scott Couper (1831-1892) pioneered the study of chemical structure. He decided that carbon atoms had a "valency" of two or four, meaning that they could form two or four bonds with other atoms. From this, he deduced that carbon atoms must be able to link up with each other. He was also the first chemist to realize that carbon atoms could bond together to form rings.

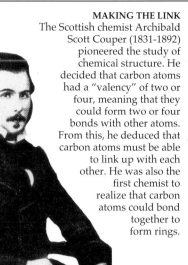

THE TETRAHEDRAL ATOM
In 1874 the Dutch chemist Jacobus van't Hoff (1852-1911) was the first person to suggest that the four bonds that a carbon atom can form might be arranged in a tetrahedral shape, like the corners of a pyramid. This shape explains why it is possible to have one carbon compound with two different forms that are like mirror images of each other. These are called isomers.

TAKING IN AND PAYING OUT
Nearly all the carbon in living things comes from carbon dioxide in the air. Energy is needed to build this carbon into complex compounds, and this energy is released when the compounds are broken down. A galloping horse gets the energy it needs to move by breaking down the carbohydrate glucose during the process of respiration (p. 18). A car gets its energy by breaking down another carbon-containing compound – petrol.

Carbon   Hydrogen   Oxygen

Palmitic acid molecule

Vegetable oil

OILS AND FATS
Vegetable oil contains substances called triglycerides – compounds that contain three long chains of carbon atoms. Each chain is made from a fatty acid, such as palmitic acid (above). Oils belong to a group of substances called lipids, which include fats and waxes. Lipids do not dissolve in water. Living things use them to store energy, to make membranes (p. 56), and to form waterproof or insulating layers.

Sites that carry oxygen

PROTEINS
A piece of meat contains large amounts of proteins, which, after nucleic acids (p. 34), are the most complicated carbon-containing substances in living things. Protein molecules have many different shapes, and the shape of each one determines the functions that it can carry out. A haemoglobin molecule, shown here, binds oxygen and carries it around the bloodstream. Other proteins build up parts of cells, make things move, attack foreign substances, or speed up chemical reactions.

Haemoglobin molecule

Cubes of meat

Life's building blocks

A<small>BOUT</small> 400 <small>YEARS AGO</small>, a revolutionary optical instrument appeared in Europe. It was the microscope, which soon became a powerful tool for investigating the natural world. One of the most talented early microscopists was the English physicist Robert Hooke (1635–1703). He built his own microscope and examined all kinds of specimens, from leaves to insects. He noticed that a thin slice of cork appeared to be made of tiny boxes, which he called cells. It took 150 years for biologists to realize that all living things – from trees to whales – are made up in the same way. Each cell is like a microscopic factory, in which conditions are always carefully regulated. A plant cell and an animal cell, shown here on facing pages, differ in important ways, but both live by harnessing energy and putting it to work. They use a range of special internal structures called organelles to do this.

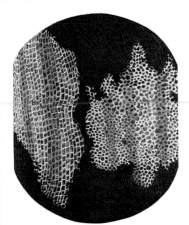

WINDOW ON A WORLD
This illustration of a slice of cork, seen under a microscope, shows its cellular structure. It appeared in Robert Hooke's book *Micrographia*, published in 1665. Hooke was a gifted artist, and he illustrated the book himself. The large leather-bound volume, with its special fold-out pages, became the 17th-century equivalent of a bestseller.

SOLAR PANELS
In 1862 the German botanist Julius von Sachs discovered green bean-shaped organelles in leaves. These are now known as chloroplasts. Each one contains stacks of tiny discs called thylakoids. A green pigment, called chlorophyll (p. 16), on the surface of the thylakoids converts the light energy into chemical energy to drive photosynthesis.

Thylakoid stack

Chloroplast

Plasma membranes

Plasmodesma

Shared cell wall

Cytoplasm

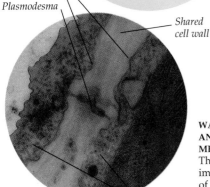

MAKING CONNECTIONS
Although separate, cells are not always cut off from each other. This electron microscope image shows a strand of cytoplasm called a plasmodesma that connects two plant cells. Plasmodesmata allow neighbouring cells to stay in chemical contact.

WALLS AND MEMBRANES
The most important part of any cell is the thin film, or plasma membrane, that separates it from the outside world. This complex double layer (p. 56) automatically seals itself if it is broken, and it is semi-permeable, allowing selected substances into or out of a cell (p. 20). Plants cells, like this one, also have a thick cellulose cell wall.

Rigid cell wall

Nucleus

Plasma membrane

Large reservoir or vacuole, filled with cell sap and surrounded by a membrane

Cytoplasm pushed outwards by pressure of cell sap in vacuole

Mitochondrion

Chloroplast

POWERING THE CELL
All cells, except those of bacteria, contain tiny "power stations" called mitochondria. This electron micrograph (p. 15) shows two mitochondria from a plant cell. These organelles work by releasing energy through a process called respiration (p.18).

FIT FOR THE JOB
On average, animal cells are about 0.01 mm (0.0004 in) across. Unlike plant cells, they do not have cell walls, chloroplasts, or vacuoles, and they vary greatly in form according to the work that they carry out. A human red blood cell, or corpuscle, is shaped like a disc with sunken faces, and it does not have a nucleus. A nerve cell consists of thread-like axons, and can be several metres long, while a hepatocyte, from the liver, is rounded and has an intricately folded surface. Animal eggs are the largest cells that exist. Before it begins to develop, the egg of an ostrich consists of one single cell that can be up to 25 cm (10 in) long. Including its shell, it can weigh over 1.5 kg (3.3 lb).

Human red blood cell or erythrocyte

Nerve cell or neuron

Axon

Cell body

Liver cell or hepatocyte

Folded surface

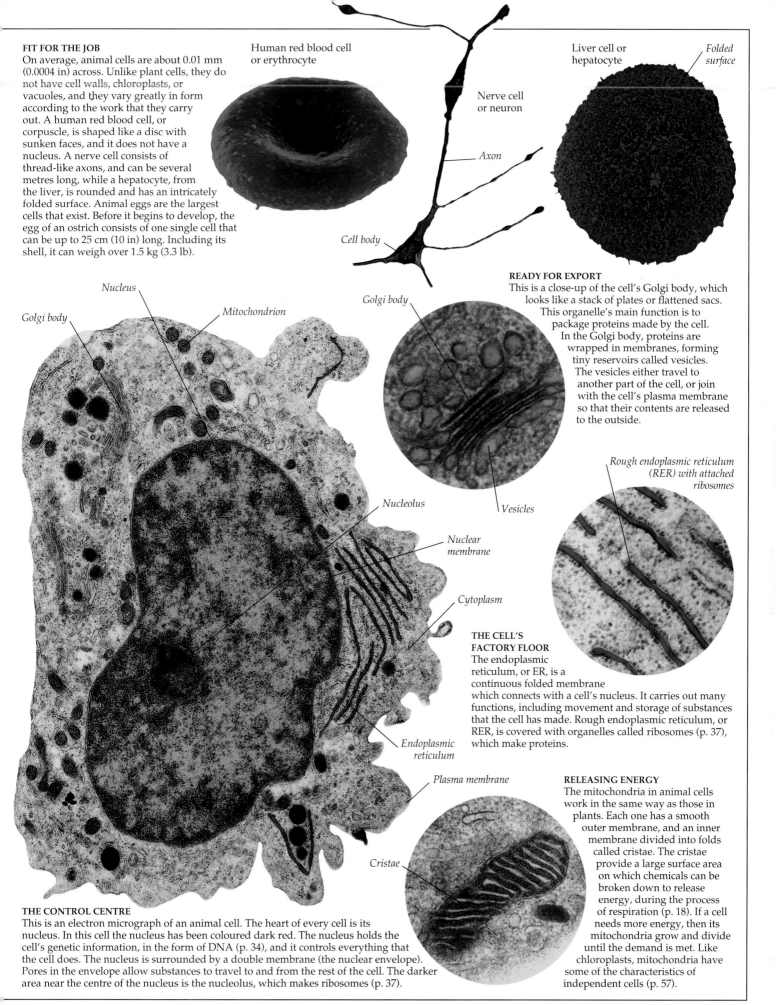

Nucleus

Golgi body

Mitochondrion

Golgi body

READY FOR EXPORT
This is a close-up of the cell's Golgi body, which looks like a stack of plates or flattened sacs. This organelle's main function is to package proteins made by the cell. In the Golgi body, proteins are wrapped in membranes, forming tiny reservoirs called vesicles. The vesicles either travel to another part of the cell, or join with the cell's plasma membrane so that their contents are released to the outside.

Rough endoplasmic reticulum (RER) with attached ribosomes

Nucleolus

Nuclear membrane

Vesicles

Cytoplasm

THE CELL'S FACTORY FLOOR
The endoplasmic reticulum, or ER, is a continuous folded membrane which connects with a cell's nucleus. It carries out many functions, including movement and storage of substances that the cell has made. Rough endoplasmic reticulum, or RER, is covered with organelles called ribosomes (p. 37), which make proteins.

Endoplasmic reticulum

Plasma membrane

Cristae

RELEASING ENERGY
The mitochondria in animal cells work in the same way as those in plants. Each one has a smooth outer membrane, and an inner membrane divided into folds called cristae. The cristae provide a large surface area on which chemicals can be broken down to release energy, during the process of respiration (p. 18). If a cell needs more energy, then its mitochondria grow and divide until the demand is met. Like chloroplasts, mitochondria have some of the characteristics of independent cells (p. 57).

THE CONTROL CENTRE
This is an electron micrograph of an animal cell. The heart of every cell is its nucleus. In this cell the nucleus has been coloured dark red. The nucleus holds the cell's genetic information, in the form of DNA (p. 34), and it controls everything that the cell does. The nucleus is surrounded by a double membrane (the nuclear envelope). Pores in the envelope allow substances to travel to and from the rest of the cell. The darker area near the centre of the nucleus is the nucleolus, which makes ribosomes (p. 37).

11

Single-celled life

THE HUMAN BODY contains over 50 million million cells that work together to perform different tasks. Most forms of life, however, consist of just a single cell that carries out all the tasks involved in staying alive. With a few exceptions, single-celled organisms are so small that they cannot be seen with the naked eye, and until the 17th century no-one had any idea that they existed. The invention of the microscope revealed that single-celled creatures live almost everywhere, from pond water to household dust. Many exist on, and even in, our own bodies. In the 20th century scientists have discovered that the many different forms of single-celled life fall into two distinct groups. Some cells are much like our own, each with a nucleus and a range of organelles. Others are far smaller and simpler, with very few internal structures. These simple organisms – the bacteria – are the most abundant life form on Earth.

Tiny lens

fig: A   D
fig: B
fig: E: fig: G.
fig: F

EXPLORING A HIDDEN WORLD
The pioneering Dutch microscopist Antoni van Leeuwenhoek (1632-1723) designed and built this small single-lens microscope. In 1683, using this instrument, he became the first person to see bacteria. He made these sketches of the movements of bacteria that he found living on his teeth.

ANCIENT LIFE
These worm-like strands, photographed in ultraviolet light, are clusters of single-celled organisms called cyanobacteria. They make their food by using sunlight (p. 16), and are the oldest living things to be found on the Earth. Geologists have discovered huge fossilized mats of cyanobacteria, called stromatolites (p. 57), that are over 3,000 million years old – almost three-quarters of the age of planet Earth itself.

MICROBES AND DISEASE
Research by the German bacteriologist Robert Koch (1843-1910) helped to prove that bacteria are one of the causes of disease. He found that certain bacteria grown from a culture in the laboratory could produce the deadly disease anthrax when introduced into cattle.

THE RACE TO REPRODUCE
A bacterium reproduces simply by dividing to make two new cells (p. 32). Under ideal conditions, each bacterium can split in two every 20 minutes. Each of these two will then do the same. Within just a few hours, a single bacterium can produce a teeming colony of millions, like the one below.

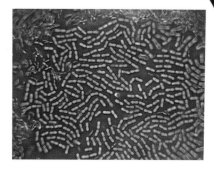

Diatom

12

LIFE IN A GLASS CASE

The circle below is a collection of fossilized diatoms, tiny plant-like organisms that are far smaller than a pinhead and invisible to the naked eye. A diatom's single cell is supported by a beautifully sculpted case (right), made of silica, a material similar to glass. The case consists of two halves that fit over each other, and each species has a case of a slightly different shape. In the 19th century the arranging of diatoms became a craze. One microscopist managed to squeeze all the diatoms then known – over 4,000 species – into a square less than 7 mm (0.3 in) across.

Filigree silica skeleton

Scanning electron micrograph of boat-shaped diatom

Desmid

Cell wall

PLANT ADRIFT

Desmids are plant-like organisms found in water that is poor in nutrients. A desmid's single cell has a narrow "waist", making it look like two cells joined together. The green colour in this light microscope image is produced by the presence of chlorophyll (p. 16) in the cell.

Pseudopod

Light microscope image of amoeba

CHANGING SHAPE

Unlike diatoms and desmids, an amoeba is a microscopic predator. Its single cell has no fixed shape, and it moves by putting out pseudopods ("false feet") into which the cytoplasm (p. 23) flows. The amoeba feeds by surrounding other organisms and engulfing them.

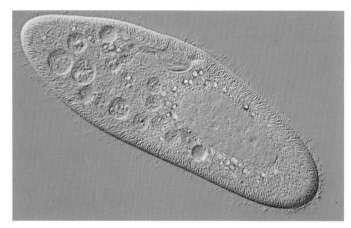

HIGH-SPEED SLIPPERS

This *Paramecium*, once called a "slipper animalcule", is one of the fastest movers in the single-celled world. It is covered with thousands of tiny hairs, or cilia, that act like microscopic oars to push it through the water. It moves so quickly that light microscopists have to add a thickening agent to the water to slow it down sufficiently to study it.

PRESERVED IN STONE

The masons of ancient Egypt built the pyramids using a kind of rock called nummilitic limestone. It is made entirely from the cases of single-celled marine organisms called foraminiferans. The rock forms when countless trillions of these microscopic skeletons build up into a thick layer on the bed of an ancient sea, and are slowly compressed.

Cells and organisms

IN MANY FORMS OF LIFE, cells do not exist on their own. Instead, they form small parts of much larger organisms. This joint approach to life has several advantages. It allows living things to grow much larger, so they are better at fending off their enemies. It also allows a division of labour, so that different cells can specialize in a particular range of tasks. In plants, for example, some cells harness the energy in light, while others carry nutrients from one place to another. In animals, some cells carry messages or supplies. Others surround themselves with a jacket of minerals to form bone. The various cells in a multicellular organism depend on each other, and are arranged in a highly ordered way. Powerful microscopes and special stains now enable scientists to investigate the different levels in this arrangement, and to see how the levels are built up to form a complete organism.

RUDOLPH VIRCHOW
In 1838 the German botanist Jakob Schleiden (1804-1881) concluded that all plants are made of cells. A year later, Theodor Schwann (1810-1882) broadened this to include all living things. The new "cell theory" was completed by Rudolf Virchow (1821-1902) in the middle of the 19th century when he stated that cells can only be made by existing cells.

From cell to organism

The human body is organized on several different levels, shown from left to right across these two pages. Cells, the lowest level, are the basic structural units of the body. Some cells, such as red blood cells, live for just a few weeks and are then replaced, but others last an entire lifetime. The next level of organization is a group of similar cells, which is known as a tissue. Several tissues join together to form an organ, and organs themselves work together to form organ systems. At the highest level of all, a collection of systems produces an organism – the body itself. In this example the organ system is the digestive system and the organ is the liver. The internal structure of the liver is shown using a method called corrosion casting.

Individual liver cell

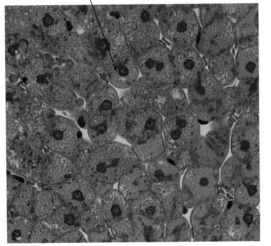

LIVER CELLS
A liver cell plays an important role in maintaining the chemical balance of the body. Among other things, it converts surplus glucose, or blood sugar, into a much less soluble storage sugar called glycogen. When the body needs glucose, it carries out the reaction in reverse.

Lobe composed of liver cells

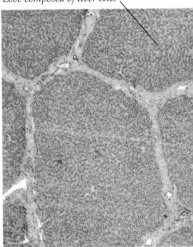

LIVER TISSUE
Vast numbers of liver cells are packed together in sheets a single cell thick, all in direct contact with blood. Unlike many of the body's tissues, liver tissue can regenerate quickly.

SLICES OF LIFE
The cells on this page have all been photographed through a light microscope. To make them visible, they have been specially prepared. Each specimen of tissue has been treated with stains, and a fine slice has then been cut from the specimen using a precision instrument called a rocking microtome. The slice is then mounted on a slide. The microtome shaves off slices that are less than one cell thick. Since each slice has very little depth, most of its details can be brought into focus at the same time.

Bottle of staining solution

Pipette

COLOUR CODING CELLS
Histologists – specialists who study the tissues of living things – use chemical stains to reveal the different structures and substances inside cells. The two slides on the right show similar cells, but they have been stained in different ways. Stains react with particular substances in the cells. Haemotoxylin, for example, is alkaline and it reacts with nucleic acids (p. 34), making cell nuclei dark.

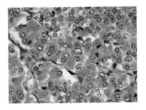

Pituitary cells stained by Slidder's trichrome method

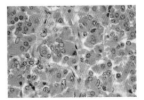

Pituitary cells stained with eosin and haemotoxylin

STUDYING CELLS

The French pathologist Marie François Bichat (1771-1802) was one of the first people to realize that organs are made of different groups of cells. He called these groups tissues, because they are often in the form of thin sheets. Although Bichat died while still young, his work helped to form a new branch of science called histology – the study of the fine structure of tissues and organs.

Fruiting body develops

Fruiting body matures

Slug migrates towards light

Spores released

Germinating spore

Independent cell

Cell mass forms

Cells attract each other by exuding a chemical

CLUBBING TOGETHER

Cellular slime moulds are strange organisms that live in a multicellular way only when conditions become difficult. When this happens, the normally independent cells gather together to form a "slug", which moves towards light. After a time, the slug produces a fruiting body. There is some division of labour, because some cells form the stalk while others form spore cases or spores. The released spores develop into new independent cells.

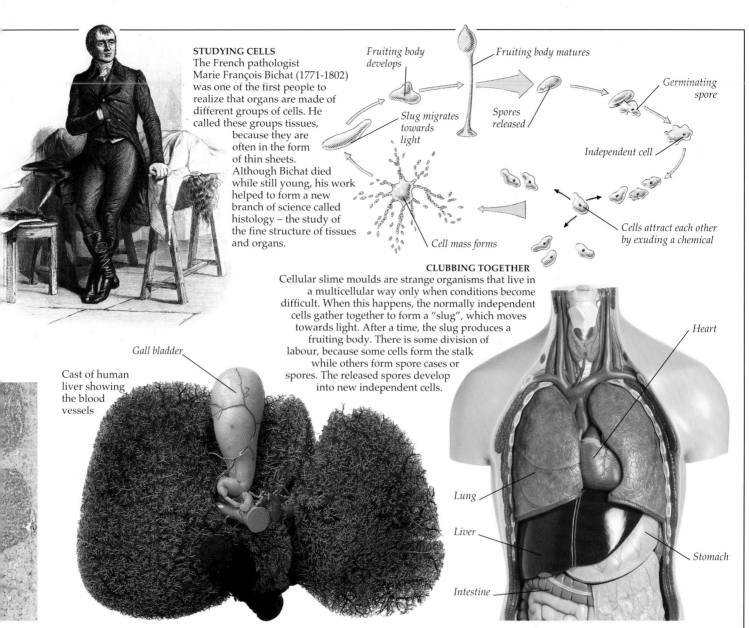

Gall bladder

Cast of human liver showing the blood vessels

Heart

Lung

Liver

Stomach

Intestine

THE LIVER

The liver is one of the largest organs in the human body. It consists of several types of tissue and is divided into two lobes. This cast shows the vessels that carry blood through the liver. The veins and venules are coloured blue, while the arteries and arterioles are red. The yellow object, which has been lifted up to reveal the liver, is the gall bladder which collects bile, a digestive fluid.

SYSTEM AND BODY

The liver forms part of the digestive system, which breaks down food for use by the body. This is just one of more than ten major systems that enable the body to stay alive. Others include the skeletal system, providing support, the nervous system, coordinating the body, and the respiratory system, supplying oxygen and getting rid of carbon dioxide.

ELECTRON VIEW

Most light microscopes cannot produce clear images at magnifications greater than about 1500. Electron microscopes (EMs) can magnify more than 50,000 times and still produce a clear picture. They work by bombarding a specimen with a beam of electrons. These pass through the specimen in a transmission electron microscope (TEM) or are reflected by its surface in a scanning electron microscope (SEM). In either case, the microscope collects the electrons and uses them to form an image. This image is black and white, but it is often artificially coloured by computer.

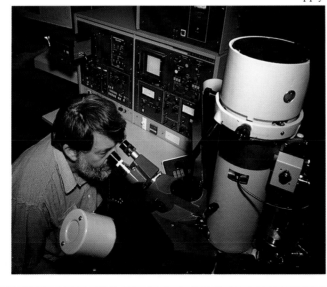

METAL-COATED CELL

This SEM image of a liver cell shows the three-dimensional structure of the outer surface. The cell has been covered with a thin layer of metal atoms to make it reflect the electrons.

Photosynthesis

Most plants are rooted in the soil, and if they are pulled up they die. These facts suggest that plants feed on soil, and for centuries this is what people believed. However, when early scientists started to investigate plants, they made some strange discoveries. The Belgian doctor Jan Baptista van Helmont (1577-1644) began by planting a small willow tree in a pot of earth, after weighing them both. Five years later he again weighed the tree and the pot. He found that while the willow had put on nearly 75 kg (165 lb), the soil was only 57 g (2 oz) lighter. Clearly, the plant had grown by using something other than soil. Helmont decided that it had fed on the water that he had given it. He was partly right, but he had overlooked another essential source of raw materials. In 1705 the English chemist Stephen Hales showed that plants also need air to grow. Scientists now know that plants absorb water from the soil and carbon dioxide from the air. Using energy from the Sun, they combine these simple raw materials to produce glucose, and from glucose they make a range of carbon-containing substances. This process is called photosynthesis, and it is the cornerstone of life on Earth.

STUDYING AIR AND WATER
The English physiologist and curate Stephen Hales (1677–1761) carried out many experiments into the movement of water through plants, and was the first person to note that plants absorb carbon dioxide from the air. In his influential book *Vegetable Staticks*, published in 1727, he set out his discoveries about the structure and functions of the parts of a plant. He also studied many aspects of animal blood systems (p. 27) and bone growth.

Fulcrum

UNRAVELLING PHOTOSYNTHESIS
Photosynthesis, by which plants convert simple inorganic molecules into larger organic ones, is a complex process, and many different scientists have played a part in finding out exactly how it takes place. The Dutch doctor Jan Ingenhousz (1730-1799) knew from the work of Stephen Hales (above right) and Joseph Priestley (opposite) that plants take in carbon dioxide. His experiments revealed that plants absorb carbon dioxide only in the presence of light. This discovery showed that light plays a key part in photosynthesis. In the dark, plants actually release carbon dioxide and take in oxygen as they carry out respiration (p. 18) to provide them with energy.

Weights

STARTING OUT
In this replica of van Helmont's experiment, the plant and pot together are initially lighter than the weights. The growing plant draws up water from the soil, in a process called transpiration, and its leaves absorb carbon dioxide from the air. The chloroplasts (p. 10) in its leaves harness the energy in sunlight, and use this energy to combine the water and carbon dioxide into glucose.

Seedling

Pot of earth

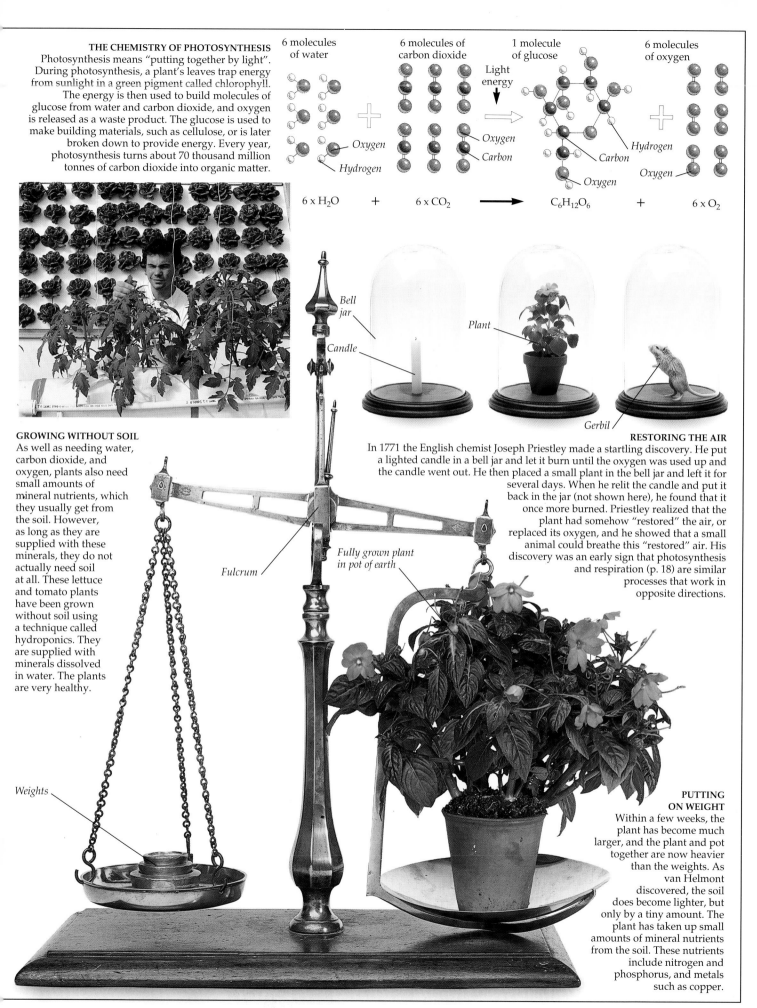

THE CHEMISTRY OF PHOTOSYNTHESIS

Photosynthesis means "putting together by light". During photosynthesis, a plant's leaves trap energy from sunlight in a green pigment called chlorophyll. The energy is then used to build molecules of glucose from water and carbon dioxide, and oxygen is released as a waste product. The glucose is used to make building materials, such as cellulose, or is later broken down to provide energy. Every year, photosynthesis turns about 70 thousand million tonnes of carbon dioxide into organic matter.

6 molecules of water

Oxygen

Hydrogen

6 molecules of carbon dioxide

Oxygen

Carbon

Light energy

1 molecule of glucose

Hydrogen

Carbon

Oxygen

6 molecules of oxygen

Oxygen

$$6 \times H_2O + 6 \times CO_2 \longrightarrow C_6H_{12}O_6 + 6 \times O_2$$

Bell jar

Candle

Plant

Gerbil

GROWING WITHOUT SOIL

As well as needing water, carbon dioxide, and oxygen, plants also need small amounts of mineral nutrients, which they usually get from the soil. However, as long as they are supplied with these minerals, they do not actually need soil at all. These lettuce and tomato plants have been grown without soil using a technique called hydroponics. They are supplied with minerals dissolved in water. The plants are very healthy.

Fulcrum

Fully grown plant in pot of earth

RESTORING THE AIR

In 1771 the English chemist Joseph Priestley made a startling discovery. He put a lighted candle in a bell jar and let it burn until the oxygen was used up and the candle went out. He then placed a small plant in the bell jar and left it for several days. When he relit the candle and put it back in the jar (not shown here), he found that it once more burned. Priestley realized that the plant had somehow "restored" the air, or replaced its oxygen, and he showed that a small animal could breathe this "restored" air. His discovery was an early sign that photosynthesis and respiration (p. 18) are similar processes that work in opposite directions.

Weights

PUTTING ON WEIGHT

Within a few weeks, the plant has become much larger, and the plant and pot together are now heavier than the weights. As van Helmont discovered, the soil does become lighter, but only by a tiny amount. The plant has taken up small amounts of mineral nutrients from the soil. These nutrients include nitrogen and phosphorus, and metals such as copper.

Respiration

Many breakthroughs in biology have been made by taking careful measurements. Jan Baptista van Helmont found out some important facts about photosynthesis (p. 16) by weighing a growing plant. More than 150 years later, the French chemist Antoine Laurent Lavoisier found out about another fundamental biochemical process by making measurements using a live guinea pig. In 1772 Lavoisier had devised a new theory of combustion, or burning. He discovered that during combustion a carbon-containing fuel combines with oxygen and produces carbon dioxide. He was struck by the similarity between combustion and the way in which animals use food. In 1783 he monitored a guinea pig's output of heat and carbon dioxide to see if the two processes were related. Lavoisier's results helped to show that animals live by slowly "burning" their food. This process is now known as respiration, and it takes place inside living cells. Respiration is the counterpart of photosynthesis. Photosynthesis uses energy to build up substances, while respiration releases energy by breaking them down.

Hair at low temperature

VICTIM OF CHANGE
Antoine Laurent Lavoisier (1743–1794) was one of the most gifted scientists of the 18th century. He discovered that air is largely a mixture of two gases, oxygen and nitrogen, and that water is a compound of oxygen and hydrogen. Despite his many achievements, he became a victim of the French Revolution and died on the guillotine.

MAKING THINGS MOVE
The human body is powered by glucose, a simple carbohydrate (p. 8) that is rich in energy. Glucose is usually broken down by aerobic respiration – a form of respiration that requires oxygen. This process extracts the maximum amount of energy from each glucose molecule and produces carbon dioxide and water as waste products. Aerobic respiration takes place inside mitochondria (p. 11). During vigorous exercise, the body's oxygen intake is stepped up by deep and rapid breathing. This also helps to get rid of the carbon dioxide waste, which is expelled in the breath.

THE LIVING FURNACE
Humans are endotherms (p. 26), which means that we keep our bodies at a constant warm temperature. The heat that maintains the temperature difference between the body and its surroundings comes mainly from respiration. These computerized thermal images show the range of skin temperature of a woman and a man. The warmest regions, coloured white, red, and orange, are at about 37 °C (98.6 °F). They are on the upper body, where most heat is generated. The coolest regions are shown here in blue and purple. Warmth helps to keep the body's metabolism, or chemical processes, running at a brisk rate. However, body temperature has to be carefully regulated (p. 26), as too much heat can permanently disrupt the structure of the body's proteins.

Hot area around body centre

Low temperature where bones are close to surface and heat loss is greatest

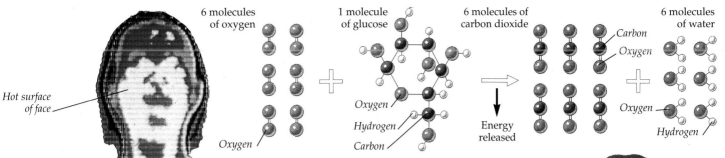

6 molecules of oxygen

Oxygen

1 molecule of glucose

Oxygen

Hydrogen

Carbon

Energy released

6 molecules of carbon dioxide

Carbon

Oxygen

6 molecules of water

Oxygen

Hydrogen

Hot surface of face

THE CHEMISTRY OF RESPIRATION
In outline, aerobic respiration is the exact opposite of photosynthesis (p. 16). A single molecule of glucose is broken down by combining it with oxygen. This produces energy, carbon dioxide and water. Unlike fire, respiration does not run out of control. Instead, it releases energy in a gradual way at a low temperature through a complex cycle of chemical reactions. Many living things can partially break down glucose without using oxygen. This is called anaerobic respiration and it releases less energy than aerobic respiration.

THE CITRIC ACID CYCLE
The German biochemist Hans Krebs (1900–1981) discovered that glucose is gradually broken down in cells in a cycle of reactions called the citric acid cycle or Krebs cycle. At each step in the cycle, a small amount of energy is released and made available to the cell.

Bubbles of carbon dioxide produced by anaerobic respiration of yeast in a sugar solution

RESPIRATION IN PLANTS
Animals do not carry out photosynthesis, but plants do carry out respiration. They use it to release stored energy. This American skunk cabbage is melting its way up through the springtime snow by releasing heat. The heat is produced by respiration. Similar plants attract pollinating insects by warming up parts of their flowers. The warmth makes chemicals evaporate, and these lure insects to the plants.

GASPING FOR BREATH
During hard exercise, muscles sometimes run out of the oxygen needed for aerobic respiration. They then partially switch over to anaerobic respiration, in which glucose is broken down to produce lactic acid. This acid eventually stops the muscles working properly and causes muscle fatigue. When oxygen becomes available, the lactic acid is broken down.

RESPIRATION WITHOUT OXYGEN
This frothing glass contains yeast in sugary water. Yeast breaks down the sugar by anaerobic respiration and produces alcohol and carbon dioxide as waste. A similar process makes bread rise. Many organisms can respire in this way.

Getting supplies

ALL LIVING THINGS constantly use up raw materials and generate waste. To stay alive, they have to obtain fresh supplies of the substances that they need, and they must get rid of waste products. These two processes are called nutrition and excretion. Living things nourish themselves in two very different ways. Autotrophs ("self-feeders") include plants and many bacteria. These take in simple inorganic nutrients; by using processes such as photosynthesis (p. 16), they combine these substances to form all the organic molecules that they need. Heterotrophs ("other-feeders"), which include all fungi and animals, cannot use such simple materials. They have to take in ready-made organic molecules. Many of these molecules are too big to pass through cell membranes (p. 59), so they have to be broken down, or digested.

THE NEED FOR NITROGEN
Plants need nitrogen, and most of them obtain it by absorbing nitrogen compounds from the soil. The French chemist Jean Baptiste Boussingault (1802-1887), a pioneer in the study of plant nutrition, discovered that plants in the pea family can use nitrogen directly from the air. They are helped by bacteria that grow in root nodules.

GOING FOR GROWTH
This devastated landscape on the Pacific island of Nauru is all that remains of one of the world's largest outcrops of rock phosphate, a natural fertilizer. Rock phosphate contains phosphorus, an element that is essential for plant growth. Phosphates are mined in many parts of the world and put on farmland to improve crop yields. Ironically, the quest for this life-giving substance has left the interior of Nauru almost totally barren.

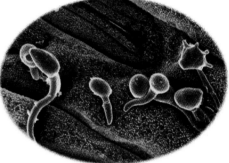

SOAKING UP FOOD
This electron micrograph shows fungal spores germinating on a leaf. The fungi grow threads, called hyphae (p. 51), that penetrate the leaf and release proteins called enzymes to digest the organic matter. The fungi then absorb the digested nutrients. Many bacteria also obtain nutrients in this way.

Greater concentration outside cell

Balanced concentration

Nucleus

Balanced concentration

Increased concentration inside cell

More concentrated solution inside cell

Water has moved in, balancing concentrations

DIFFUSION
Nutrition and excretion both involve moving substances across cell membranes (p. 59). This can happen in three ways. In simple diffusion, molecules move from a region of high concentration to one of low concentration, balancing the concentration on both sides of the membrane. This requires no energy input from the cell.

ACTIVE TRANSPORT
All cells can move a variety of substances "uphill", so that they become more concentrated on one side of the cell membrane than on the other. This process is called active transport. Unlike diffusion, active transport requires energy, and it often involves special carrier proteins.

OSMOSIS
Cell membranes are permeable to water, but impermeable to many dissolved substances, or solutes. During osmosis, water molecules travel through a membrane towards the side containing the highest concentration of solutes. Osmosis is a form of diffusion. It requires no energy input from the cell.

Leaves use light to create carbohydrates from simple raw materials

Slug consumes plant

Soil supplies some nutrients to plant

FIRST LINK
Food and energy move between species in a sequence called a food chain. Almost all food chains begin with a plant. Plants are known as "producers", because they manufacture food from inorganic raw materials. Here, the food made by a plant is being eaten by slugs. The slugs are primary consumers, because they are the first animals in this chain to make use of the plant food. A slug uses up most of its food to power its body, with just a small amount being used to form living tissue. Only this part of the food can be passed on up the chain.

LIVING WITHOUT WATER

All animals need to take in water, but not all animals need to drink. Gerbils live in deserts and, like many desert rodents, they can get all the water they require from their food. They use the "metabolic" water that is released when food is broken down by respiration (p. 18). They lose very little water through their skin and lungs, and only a small amount in their urine.

LITTLE AND LARGE

The basking shark is the world's second-largest fish, and can reach a length of 10 m (33 ft). Like many whales, it is a filter feeder, and lives by sieving food from the sea. A basking shark cruises close to the surface with its mouth open, collecting vast quantities of tiny planktonic organisms with its sieve-like gills. Although its food is small, it is extremely abundant and easy to catch. This allows the shark to grow to a great size.

LYING IN WAIT

Animals use two basic strategies for getting food – they either track it down or they wait for it to come their way. This underwater web (above) has been created by a caddisfly larva. It uses the second strategy, waiting at the base of the web and eating any small animals swept in by the current. Larvae that move about to find food may find more, but they use more energy and risk being eaten.

Chains of life

Plants are the great providers for life on Earth. By building up organic matter from simple raw materials, they generate a supply of food that can be passed on through chains of living things. A typical "food chain" begins when a plant is eaten by an animal. The food is passed on when the animal is eaten, and it carries on up the chain until it reaches a top predator – a carnivorous animal that has no natural enemies. When this animal dies, the substances in its body are recycled by bacteria and fungi, and they can be used by plants once again. The food chain shown here has just four links, but even the longest food chains rarely have more than six links. This is because animals use most of their food to power their bodies. Towards the end of a food chain, hardly any food is left to be passed on.

END OF THE LINE

In this food chain the badger, which eats slow-worms, is the tertiary consumer, because it gets its food "third-hand". A live adult badger is rarely eaten by other animals, so it brings this chain to an end. Badgers eat both plant and animal food, so the same badger will also be involved in many other food chains, often at different levels. Together, the food chains in a living community form a complex food web.

THE GO-BETWEEN

A slow-worm is a small lizard without legs. It hunts other animals, and slugs are a favourite target. Here, the slow-worm is a secondary consumer, because it gets "second-hand" food. Secondary consumers are usually bigger than primary consumers and there are usually fewer of them. In food chains that involve parasites (p. 46), this situation can be reversed.

Getting around

In the late 1930s Albert von Szent-Györgi, a Hungarian biochemist, mixed together two proteins in a laboratory experiment. Upon adding a few drops of a third chemical, he witnessed an extraordinary event. The dissolved mixture suddenly contracted – almost as if it had come to life. Szent-Györgi's experiment is one of many that have helped to show exactly what makes living things move. The two proteins that he used were actin and myosin, which are found in muscles, and the substance that he added to them was adenosine triphosphate, or ATP, an energy carrier used by all living things. Together, the actin and myosin turn chemical energy into movement, and it is the coordinated movements of billions of actin and myosin molecules that allow a fish to swim, a bird to fly, and a snake to slither across the ground. Since the 1930s biochemists have found out that these proteins – or ones very much like them – are found not only in muscles, but in almost all cells. By pulling together, they can move anything, from an amoeba to an elephant.

PULLING POWER
Muscles make up about half a pigeon's body weight. Muscles can pull but they cannot push, so each muscle or set of muscles is opposed by another that pulls in the opposite direction. Like all vertebrates, a pigeon has two main types of muscle tissue. Striated or skeletal muscles, which are attached to the bones, move parts of the body relative to each other. Smooth or visceral muscles, which are attached to the internal organs, move food through the digestive system, and keep the body in a stable state (p. 26).

THE BENDING BACKBONE
When a skink walks, its body snakes from side to side. This happens because muscles on either side of its body contract alternately, throwing its backbone into a curve and bringing its feet forwards to take a step. This snaking way of moving evolved long ago in the history of vertebrates, and is still used by many fish, amphibians and reptiles. Some mammals, such as dogs, move in a different way, by making their backbones bend up and down.

Paramecium

STRETCH AND RELAX
An earthworm does not have any hard body parts, but the pressure of its body fluid forms a "hydrostatic skeleton" that its muscles can pull against. Each fluid-filled segment has two sets of muscles that work against each other. One set runs along the segment, and when it contracts, the segment becomes shorter and fatter. The other set runs around the segment. When this set contracts, it squeezes the segment and it lengthens. Waves of muscle contraction make the worm move in a coordinated way.

SWIMMING WITH CILIA
Like many single-celled organisms (p. 13), microscopic *Paramecium* moves by beating thousands of tiny hairs called cilia. If it hits an obstacle, these cilia immediately go into reverse. The cell then changes angle slightly and moves forwards once more. This simple sequence of movements is enough to prevent *Paramecium* from being trapped by the objects around it.

Algal filaments

FAST AND SLOW MUSCLES
A dogfish swims by using two types of striated muscle. "Slow" muscle takes a long time to tire and is used for steady swimming. "Fast" muscle is used for a sudden burst of speed when pursuing prey.

PASSIVE MOVEMENT

Plants do not have muscles, but all of them can move certain parts of themselves. They do this by growing, or by causing cells to change shape by osmosis (p. 20), changing internal pressure. Some plants can actually move about, although not under their own power. These North American tumbleweeds have been blown along by the wind, and have piled up against a fence. Once a tumbleweed has flowered, it dries up and dies. Its roots wither away and the dead plant then rolls along over open ground, scattering seeds as it goes.

Hip joint

Muscles

Kneecap

Tendons

MUSCLES AND ENERGY

Albert von Szent-Györgi (1893-1986) is remembered for his pioneering work on vitamin C, as well as for his research on muscle contraction. Some of his discoveries helped Hans Krebs (p. 19) to understand how cells generate energy from glucose during respiration.

RELAXED MUSCLE

Under very high magnification, striated muscle has light and dark bands arranged in a regular way. According to the sliding filament theory, developed in the 1950s, these bands are formed by parallel filaments of the proteins actin and myosin, arranged like the layers in a sandwich. When the muscle is resting, these stacks overlap only slightly.

Thick filaments of myosin

Thin filaments of actin

CONTRACTED MUSCLE

When a nerve (p. 25) triggers a muscle, the myosin filaments form cross-bridges with the actin filaments. Using energy from ATP, the cross-bridges repeatedly flip backwards like microscopic paddles, "rowing" the myosin filaments in between the actin filaments. The filaments slide past each other and the muscle contracts. When the nerve stops triggering the muscle, the cross-bridges break and the muscle relaxes.

OUTSIDE VIEW

The Flemish anatomist Andreas Vesalius (1514-1564) was one of the first people to investigate the detailed structure of the human body and its muscles. This woodcut from his book *De Humani Corporis Fabrica*, published in 1543, depicts a carefully dissected leg. It shows the tough tendons connecting the muscles of the lower leg to the foot.

JUMPING INTO LIFE

In the 18th century the Italian anatomist Luigi Galvani (1737-1798) discovered that the legs of a dead frog twitched when pegged to an iron frame by brass pins. He had unknowingly created an electrical circuit, indicating that contractions of the muscles are triggered by electrical charges.

MAKING A LEAP

The muscles in a frog's legs are made of many separate cells, or fibres, packed closely together. Each fibre contains smaller threads called myofibres, and these contain parallel filaments of actin and myosin. The force produced by the muscle depends on the proportion of fibres that contract simultaneously. The frog can adjust this proportion to produce enough force for a small hop or a large jump.

Sensing the world

THE WORLD AROUND US is always changing. Some of these changes, such as the rising and setting of the Sun and the passing of the seasons, take place gradually and in a rhythmic way. Others are much more sudden and unpredictable. For animals in particular, the ability to respond to change is essential. A passing shadow can herald the approach of a predator and mortal danger, while a slight vibration, or an airborne scent, can signal the chance of a meal. In order to react to the world around them, animals use their senses. People often speak of "the five senses" – meaning vision, hearing, touch, taste, and smell – but senses are actually much more varied than this. Humans are also sensitive to gravity, acceleration, and heat. Some animals can detect humidity, electrical fields, magnetic fields, and even infrared radiation. Information from the senses is gathered by special cells called nerves. Some of the incoming information is collected by simple nerve endings, while some is collected through special sense organs, such as eyes and ears. Other nerves then analyse the information that has been collected, and a further set of nerves triggers the body into action, often by causing muscles to contract (p. 23). Until the 18th century, nerves were thought to carry some kind of fluid. They are now known to conduct something quite different – electrical impulses.

LIVING COMPASSES
In 1975 scientists discovered that some marsh-dwelling bacteria can sense the direction of the Earth's magnetic field. Each bacterium has a string of iron-bearing particles that act like a compass. The bacteria are too small to be able to sense gravity, but by following the "lines of force" of the magnetic field, they can burrow downwards into the sediment that provides them with a suitable environment.

SEEING WITH SOUND
Bats hunt insects by sending out high-pitched sounds and listening for the returning echoes. The echoes enable a bat to pinpoint its prey, even in complete darkness. This system, called echolocation, is also used by dolphins, shrews, and two species of cave-dwelling birds. The sounds used in echolocation are usually far too high for us to hear.

FEELING THE WAY
Insects and other arthropods use antennae, or "feelers", to investigate their surroundings. The antennae of this longhorn beetle are much longer than its body, and are used mainly for touch. Other insects have antennae that sense airborne chemicals, sometimes in minute quantities (p. 44). Antennae that do this are often feathery, which gives them a large surface area for collecting scent molecules from the air.

Head

Thorax

Antenna

Abdomen

Multiple eyes

Lateral line

Mandibles

SENSING PRESSURE
The horizontal line along the side of this young chub is a sensory organ called the lateral line. It consists of a fluid-filled tube with small pores that open to the outside. Vibrations in the water pass into the tube and shake sensitive hairs embedded in jelly, stimulating nerve endings. This enables the fish to sense the movement of neighbouring fish or of other animals. Vibrations in the water warn the fish of a rapidly-approaching predator. Fish that swim in shoals also use their lateral lines to stay together. When one fish turns, the others detect the movement and follow suit.

DOUBLE TAKE
Jumping spiders rely on vision to catch their prey. They have several sets of eyes that work together to give the spider a sense of depth, so that it can judge distances when making a jump. Like many hunting animals, the spider is good at spotting movement, but not nearly so good at recognizing the shape of stationary prey. This kind of perception requires a much more complex brain than the spider possesses. Even a hunting mammal, such as a fox, will overlook visible food if it is downwind and keeps perfectly still.

Tip removed – growth stops *Tip replaced – growth continues* *Auxin in block produces growth upwards or to side*

Agar block absorbs auxin from removed tip

FACING THE LIGHT
Plants respond to the world around them through growth movements called tropisms, and seedlings normally bend towards the light – an example of phototropism. In 1926 the physiologist Frits Went experimented with oat seedlings and found that their tips produce a substance now called auxin, which stimulates growth. When the light shines from one side, auxin is produced on the dark side of the plant, stimulating growth and causing the plant to bend towards the light.

Nose *Eyes*
Whiskers
Ears

Moving messages

Nerve cells, or neurons, are like wires running through an animal's body. Instead of carrying an electrical current, they carry short-lived electrical impulses. A typical nerve cell has a long slender filament, called an axon, and a number of much shorter filaments that are in contact with other nerves. The nerve constantly pumps sodium out through its membrane. This creates an electrical imbalance across the membrane, called a resting potential. When the nerve is triggered, sodium rushes back across the membrane and the resting potential collapses. This triggers a chain reaction, sending an electrical impulse racing along the axon. When it arrives at the end of the axon, the impulse can then trigger another nerve.

NERVES AND MUSCLES
The Swiss physician Albrecht von Haller (1708-1777) carried out a number of experiments on nerves and muscles, and showed that stimulating a nerve would make a muscle contract. From this he correctly deduced that nerves control all the body's muscles.

ON THE ALERT
A complex nervous system keeps this meerkat alert to all the opportunities and hazards that it faces in its daily life. Its brain receives information from many different senses and uses this to update constantly its image of the body and its surroundings. On the basis of this information, it instructs the body to respond appropriately to its changing world.

Brain

Spinal cord

Peripheral nerves

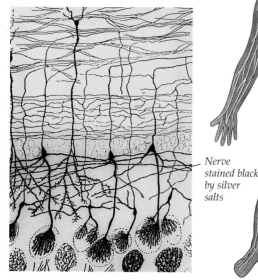

Nerve stained black by silver salts

WORKING TOGETHER
The human nervous system contains about 10 billion cells. They meet at narrow gaps, called synapses, where electrical impulses are passed from one nerve to another. Sensory neurons collect information and carry it to the spinal cord and brain. Association neurons process the information and trigger motor neurons to make muscles contract.

MAKING NERVES VISIBLE
In the 1870s the Italian histologist Camillo Golgi (1844-1926) developed a staining technique that shows the fine details of individual nerve cells. Golgi's stain was improved by the Spanish histologist Santiago Ramón y Cajal (1852-1934), who made the drawing shown here. Ramón y Cajal showed that nerves meet, but do not actually join together.

Keeping a balance

EVERY YEAR, ARCTIC TERNS carry out an epic journey. These small birds leave the seas bordering the Antarctic and fly almost halfway round the world to reach the Arctic tundra. Here they raise their young, before flying all the way back. During their flight, they experience a remarkable variety of climates, but whether they are in the tropics or the polar regions, their body temperature stays at almost exactly 40 °C (104 °F). This extraordinary internal steadiness is an example of the maintenance of a constant internal environment, or "homeostasis". Homeostasis is essential to living things because the chemistry of life works most effectively in very precise conditions. Not all living things maintain a steady temperature, but all keep an internal chemical balance that is quite different from the one in the world around them. In the simplest organisms, this balance is maintained inside a single cell. In more complex forms of life, special systems monitor and adjust the balance inside an entire organism. In animals, these systems are controlled in two connected ways – by nerves (p. 25), and by special chemical messengers called hormones. Hormones often work in pairs that have opposite effects. Through a system called negative feedback, they automatically reverse any drift away from the stable state.

CENTRAL HEATING
All animals produce heat through respiration (p. 18). In mammals and birds this heat is kept in by a layer of fur, fat, or feathers. By adjusting the rate at which heat is lost, these endothermic, or "warm-blooded", animals stay at a steady warm temperature. Humans have developed artificial ways of controlling heat loss.

DRIVEN TO DRINK
About 75 per cent of a mammal's body is made up of water. If blood contains too much or too little water, the body's cells can be damaged. The concentration of a zebra's blood is monitored and adjusted by nerves and hormones. The hormones operate a negative feedback system. One hormone reduces the production of urine, and another increases it. Together, they keep the blood's water content at the right level.

THE STABLE STATE
The idea of homeostasis was first put forward by the French physiologist Claude Bernard (1813-1878). Homeostasis involves a huge range of activities. These include getting supplies (p. 20), disposing of waste, and fighting infections (p. 28). In the broadest sense, it also includes avoiding being eaten (p. 46).

MAKING ADJUSTMENTS
Like all reptiles, a lizard is ectothermic or "cold-blooded". This does not mean that its body is always cold, but that its temperature rises and falls with that of its surroundings. A lizard needs to be warm to move about, and it heats up its body by basking in the sunshine. If it gets too hot, it retreats into the shade. Butterflies also adjust their body temperature in this way.

Lizard's body absorbs heat from sunlight

Materials on the move

In large organisms, special transport systems are needed to ferry substances about and maintain the body's chemical balance. In vertebrates, the principal transport system is the bloodstream. Blood is a remarkable and very complex fluid, and it carries out many different functions. It transports dissolved oxygen and carbon dioxide, so that all the body's cells can carry out respiration (p. 18). It supplies nutrients, removes waste, and carries heat from one part of the body to another. The bloodstream serves as a communication system as well, carrying hormones from the cells where they are made to the cells where they have an effect. Blood also combats infections (p. 28), and seals any leaks in the system by clotting.

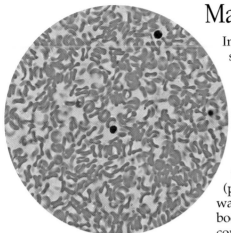

SOUP OF CELLS
This light micrograph shows a thin film of red blood cells, which carry oxygen. The two cells that are stained blue are white blood cells, which combat infections (p. 28). Half the volume of blood consists of a yellow liquid called plasma, which carries dissolved substances such as carbon dioxide, glucose, salts, and hormones.

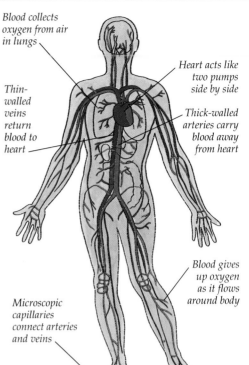

Blood collects oxygen from air in lungs

Heart acts like two pumps side by side

Thin-walled veins return blood to heart

Thick-walled arteries carry blood away from heart

Blood gives up oxygen as it flows around body

Microscopic capillaries connect arteries and veins

CHARTING THE CIRCULATION
The Arab doctor Ibn An-Nafis, who died in 1288, was the first person to describe how blood circulates through the lungs. However, his work did not become known in Europe until much later. In 1628 the English doctor William Harvey (1578-1657) published a full account of how the blood circulates around the body. Harvey could not see the extremely fine capillaries that connect arteries and veins, but he correctly guessed their existence.

William Harvey

ON THE DOUBLE
Blood is pumped by the heart and travels in closed tubes called blood vessels. In the human body, blood flows through two separate circuits, one after the other. In the pulmonary circulation, blood travels through the lungs, where it collects oxygen and gives up carbon dioxide. It then returns to the heart and is pumped around the body in the systemic circulation. During this circuit, it gives up its oxygen and takes up carbon dioxide. It takes about a minute for a single blood cell to complete the entire journey.

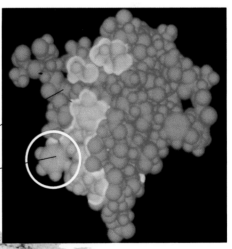

Surface of insulin molecule

Receptor site

HOW HORMONES WORK
This computer-generated image shows a single molecule of the hormone insulin. Together with another hormone, called glucagon, it keeps blood glucose levels stable. Like all hormones, insulin attaches itself to special receptors on the membranes of its target cells. In the case of insulin, this triggers a change in the target cell's chemistry, so that it takes in more glucose than before. The ringed part of the molecule shows the part that attaches to a receptor.

Attack and defence

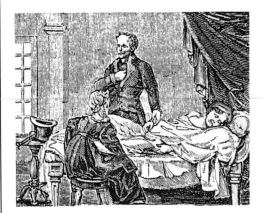

THE MYSTERIES OF DISEASE
At one time, people had little idea what caused disease. Influenza, or 'flu, was thought to be produced by an astral "influence", while malaria was thought to be caused by "bad air" rising from swamps and marshes. The work of Pasteur and Koch (p. 12) in the 19th century led doctors to realize that infectious diseases are caused by microorganisms. Non-infectious illnesses are often caused by metabolic disorders or by the immune system turning on the body itself.

ROVING DESTROYER
Rod-shaped bacteria called *Escherichia coli* normally live harmlessly in the intestines. In this dramatic electron micrograph they have entered the blood system and are being attacked by a form of white blood cell called a macrophage. White blood cells play a key role in defending the body against attack. They can move by changing shape, rather like amoebae (p. 13). They stick to the walls of tiny blood vessels called capillaries, and they squeeze through these to reach a site where bacteria are invading and causing an infection. Once a white blood cell has engulfed a number of bacteria, it dies. Large accumulations of dead white blood cells form the milky fluid called pus.

Macrophage

Thread-like pseudopods

An animal's body is home to vast numbers of bacteria. Most of them do no harm, and some bacteria in the digestive system actually help to release nutrients from food. However, if "foreign" life-forms manage to break through into the body's living tissues, they can multiply rapidly, causing a breakdown in the body's normally stable state – in other words, disease. Disease-causing agents are called pathogens. They include not only bacteria, but also several other forms of microscopic life, such as protozoans and fungi (pp. 52-3). Some diseases are caused by viruses (pp. 7 and 58), which become "alive" only once they have invaded living tissue. Animals have evolved many ways to combat attacks by pathogens. In vertebrates, the first line of defence consists of barriers such as skin, toxic chemicals, and special roving cells. If these defences are breached, a quite different form of defence comes into action. Known as the immune system, this targets individual invaders by identifying their chemical "fingerprint" and then selecting a suitable chemical weapon from over 10 million special proteins. Like an expert detective, the immune system never forgets a "face", and this makes it much harder for an intruder to stage a second attack.

*Rod-shaped
Escherichia coli
bacteria*

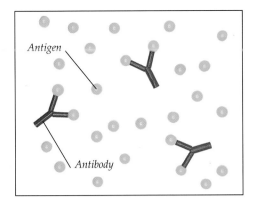

Antigen

Antibody

IMMUNE SYSTEM IN ACTION

If a microorganism manages to breach the body's general defences, it triggers the immune system into action. The immune system works by recognizing "foreign" substances, or antigens, on the surface of the intruder. These are shown here in yellow.

1 In humoral immunity, Y-shaped proteins called antibodies lock on to the antigen. Ten million different types of antibody are produced by B cells, and each of them locks on to a particular antigen.

2 As the infection continues, the invader triggers the immune system to make more of the cells that produce the appropriate antibodies. Each antibody has at least two antigen-binding sites, and locks on to the antigens on the invader's surface. By binding with antigens, the antibodies alter the invader's chemistry. This inactivates viruses, and often makes bacteria burst open. Special cells then destroy the remains.

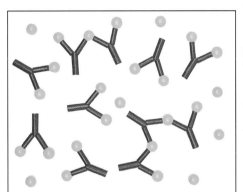

3 The first attack triggers the production of special "memory T" cells, which can remain alive for many years. When the same invader attacks the body again, the memory T cells quickly develop into cells that produce the appropriate antibodies. This kind of immune response is extremely rapid, and the memory system creates "immunity" to many common diseases.

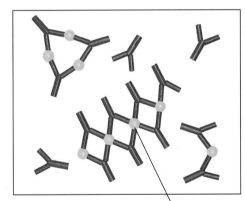

Antigen locked up by antibodies

Thymus gland produces immune system cells

Ducts empty lymph into veins near the heart

Spleen destroys bacteria and produces cells that make antibodies

Lymph nodes

Valves prevent lymph flowing backwards

SCREENING THE BODY

The lymphatic system is a collection of one-way drainage channels that reach throughout the entire body. The channels collect fluid from the spaces between cells, screen it, and then empty it into the bloodstream. The system plays an important role in defending the body because it contains large numbers of macrophages, and also special cells involved in the two kinds of immune system action (see below). Most of the screening takes place in small swellings called lymph nodes. During an infection, the nodes close to the infected site often swell up. The thymus gland and spleen are part of the lymphatic system.

Blood and immunity

Blood plays a key role, through immunity, in protecting the body against attack. It contains white cells that produce antibodies, and other white cells that engulf invaders and destroy them. Together, the two branches of the immune system – known as humoral and cellular immunity – disable most invaders. However, this extraordinary system of chemical defences is not entirely foolproof.

Antibodies in the blood sometimes attack the body itself, and the immune system can also create problems after organ transplants and blood transfusions by attacking "foreign" cells. Some viruses – for example Human Immunodeficiency Virus (HIV) – manage to escape destruction by attacking the system itself.

TAKING A CHANCE

This 17th-century engraving shows a primitive blood transfusion, with a man exchanging blood with a dog. Early transfusions – even between people – were highly dangerous, because immune reactions can make red blood cells agglutinate, or clump together. This can block small blood vessels, damaging vital organs.

ANTIGENS IN BLOOD

This electron micrograph shows red and white blood cells gathered at the site of an infection. Red blood cells have characteristic antigens, while blood plasma contains antibodies that can bind with the antigens of foreign red blood cells, making them clump. People of the same blood group have the same antigens and antibodies and can exchange blood without clumping occurring.

GROUPING BLOOD

In 1900 the Austrian Karl Landsteiner (1868-1943) showed that blood plasma from one person will often make another person's blood cells clump together. He found that people's blood falls into four main groups, now known as O, A, B, and AB, and he determined which of these groups were compatible during transfusions.

Growth and development

Mᴀɴʏ ʟɪᴠɪɴɢ ᴛʜɪɴɢs ʙᴇɢɪɴ ʟɪꜰᴇ ᴀs ᴀ sɪɴɢʟᴇ ᴄᴇʟʟ, from which a new and independent organism slowly takes shape. This remarkable sequence of events is the result of two different but closely linked processes. The first of these is growth, which is simply an increase in size. The second is development, which is an increase in complexity. Cells work best when they are of a particular size, so living things usually grow by making more cells, rather than by enlarging the cells that they already have. New cells are made by cell division, and this can happen in two ways. One form of division, called meiosis, is used only in sexual reproduction (p. 38). Another form, which is often called mitosis, is used for growth. Mitosis involves the cell nucleus splitting in two. The rest of the cell then divides, and two new cells are produced. Early on in life, cell division occurs at a very rapid rate and millions or billions of new cells can quickly build up. These new cells gradually begin to differentiate, or develop different characteristics, and eventually a mature organism is formed. When this organism reproduces, the next generation is brought into being, and the cycle of growth and development begins all over again.

THE START OF LIFE
A beech seed contains a plant embryo and a supply of food.

SPAWN TO TADPOLE
During the first days of its life, a frog's egg develops from a single cell to become a complex organism.

1 A frog begins life as a single fertilized egg cell surrounded by a coat of jelly. The lower half of the cell contains a supply of food in the form of yolk.

2 The single egg cell begins to divide. This process, which is called cleavage, is repeated about every 30 minutes. To begin with, the cells divide together, but they soon get out of step.

3 After about six hours, the egg is transformed into a fluid-filled ball called a blastula, consisting of about 10,000 cells. The ball then folds in on itself creating a gastrula, which has three different layers of cells.

4 After 24 hours, the gastrula elongates and a groove develops on its upper surface. The groove closes over to form a nerve tube. The gastrula has now become an embryo, with a distinct head and tail.

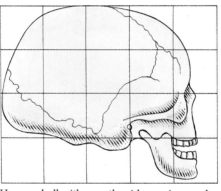

Human skull with growth grid superimposed

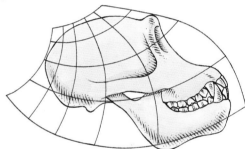

Chimpanzee skull, with growth grid adjusted

PATTERNS OF GROWTH
During development, groups of cells often divide at different rates. This is called allometric growth, and it creates the characteristic proportions of an adult organism. In 1917 the Scottish biologist D'Arcy Thompson (1860-1948) published a classic study called *On Growth and Form*, analysing allometric growth. He found that small differences in growth rates can produce large physical differences. These drawings show how the skulls of a human, chimpanzee, and baboon can be "transformed" into each other by applying different growth rates to different regions.

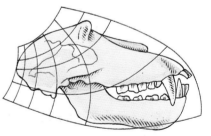

Baboon skull, with growth grid adjusted

5 The head now begins to appear, together with gill arches and the beginnings of a mouth. Internal organs are rapidly taking shape.

Gill arches

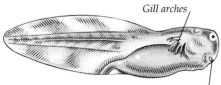

Mouth

6 After about 10 days, the tadpole is almost fully formed. It is still little bigger than the original egg, but during the next few weeks it will grow rapidly to become a frog.

KEEPING IN SHAPE
Many mollusc shells show the opposite of allometric growth. They get bigger as they get older, but their overall proportions stay exactly the same. The space inside increases as the shell gets bigger, so the occupant can use the same shell for the whole of its life. Arthropod animals such as ladybirds (opposite) have hard jointed cases that cover the whole of their bodies. In order to grow, they must periodically shed their body case, or moult. A bigger case replaces the old one.

Ladybirds mate
and females
lay eggs

Egg batch laid on leaf

Each egg cell divides
and embryos develop

CYCLES OF LIFE

We gradually change in proportion as we grow up, but many other living things undergo a rapid change in shape at some period in their lives. This is known as metamorphosis. Metamorphosis is very widespread in the animal world, and it is particularly easy to see in insects such as beetles. Like all beetles, a ladybird shows "complete" metamorphosis, meaning that its young, or larvae, look quite unlike their parents. A ladybird larva has no wings; it feeds by clambering over plants and searching out aphids. After living like this for several weeks, it forms a resting stage called a pupa. Inside the pupal case, most of the larva's cells are destroyed, to be replaced by new cells that form an adult body. Unlike the larva, the adult has wings, and this enables it to travel to new sources of food. Many other insects show "incomplete" metamorphosis. Their shape changes gradually with each moult.

Young larvae
break their way
out of the eggs

Adult ladybird flies
to new plants and
feeds on aphids

Larva has no
wings; bold
colours warn
birds that it tastes
unpleasant

Elytra gradually harden
and become spotted

Adult ladybird emerges from
pupal case; at first its wing
covers (elytra) are yellow

After several weeks, each
larva forms a pupa

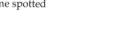

STICKING TO A PLAN

Unusually for an animal, this tiny nematode worm, called *Caenorhabditis elegans*, always has exactly the same number of cells in its adult body. Biologists have now built up a "family tree" of all its 959 cells, showing how each one originates and what it does. The tree shows that 131 of its cells are genetically programmed to die during the process of development. Over 300 of the surviving cells are used to form the nervous system. Most animals have far more cells than this, and few follow such a rigid pattern of development.

ENDLESS GROWTH

A beech seed (opposite) takes about 50 years to develop into a young tree that can reproduce but, like most plants, it does not stop growing then. It continues to grow until it is eventually blown down or killed by disease. Some animals, such as reptiles, also show "indeterminate" growth, getting bigger throughout their lives, but most birds and mammals have "determinate" growth. They stop growing once they reach a certain size.

DNA – the essence of life

SPELLING OUT A MESSAGE
This man is receiving a Morse code message of dots and dashes. The DNA message is also coded, having "letters" in the form of chemicals called bases. Like letters, the four types of bases can be arranged in an infinite number of different sequences.

IN 1869 A YOUNG SWISS DOCTOR named Friedrich Miescher (1844–1895) scraped some white blood cells from a bandage and made a curious discovery. He found that the cell nuclei contained a complex but unknown substance. Interestingly, a similar substance turned up in very different cells, such as those from fish and even fungi. The chemical became known as nucleic acid. By 1929, scientists had discovered that there were actually two kinds of nucleic acid. One of these contained the sugar ribose, and became known as ribonucleic acid, or RNA. Some RNA molecules were quite short, and they were often found outside cell nuclei. The other chemical, containing the sugar deoxyribose, became known as deoxyribonucleic acid or DNA. It was found in chromosomes (p. 36), its molecules were often extremely long, and they seemed to carry inherited characteristics from one cell to another. Gradually, it became apparent that DNA contained the entire "blueprint" of living things, written in a form that was, at the time, indecipherable. As well as holding information, DNA could also copy it, allowing the information to be passed from cell to cell. The search to find out exactly how DNA does this led to one of the most exciting and important discoveries of the 20th century, and revealed the chemical basis of life itself.

Nitrogenous base
Deoxyribose
Molecule containing phosphorus

NUCLEOTIDES
DNA consists of millions of small units called nucleotides. Each nucleotide has three parts – a sugar called deoxyribose, a molecule containing phosphorus, and a chemical called a nitrogenous base.

THE DOUBLE HELIX
In most forms of DNA, the nucleotide units form two strands that are held together by base-pairs and spiral around each other in a shape called a double helix. The sequence of base-pairs makes up the DNA's stored instructions, or code. This model shows less than 30 base-pairs. At this scale, at least a million pages would be needed to show one complete DNA molecule from a human cell.

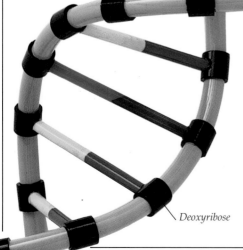

Deoxyribose

Adenine-thymine base-pair

Guanine-cytosine base-pair

"Backbone" made of alternating deoxyribose and phosphate units

BACTERIAL DNA
This electron micrograph, which is enlarged over 15,000 times, shows a molecule of DNA spilling out of a specially treated bacterium. Bacteria have no nuclei, and usually have a single circular molecule of DNA. This is spread throughout the cell. The DNA of this bacterium contains about 4 million base-pairs. Stretched out, the entire DNA molecule is about 1.5 mm (0.06 in) long, which is about 1,000 times longer than the cell itself.

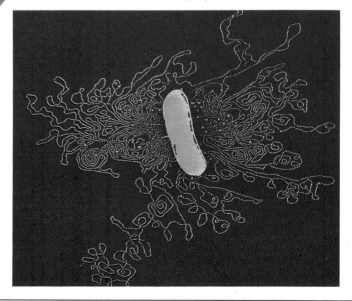

THE STRUCTURE OF DNA

In 1953 James Watson and Francis Crick made a crucial breakthrough. They correctly worked out the double helix structure of the DNA molecule. They realized that because the bases "pair", the two strands are "complementary" – rather like a negative and positive in photography. When a cell divides, the strands separate, and each one makes itself a new partner.

Phosphate-containing molecule

PAVING THE WAY

One way to investigate the structure of a chemical is to crystallize it, and then fire X-rays through the crystals. The crystals bend, or diffract, the X-rays, creating a pattern that can be analysed. In 1952 the English physicist Rosalind Franklin (1920-1958) used this technique to study DNA. Her conclusion that DNA molecules must be helical provided valuable evidence for Watson and Crick. Franklin died at the age of 38, long before her work was fully acknowledged.

Thymine   Adenine

Cytosine   Guanine

Replicating DNA

A cell's DNA contains a full set of instructions that control the way the cell works. Before a cell divides, these instructions are normally duplicated, so that a complete set can be handed on to each new cell. This process is called replication. It involves the DNA "unzipping" and unwinding to form two new molecules. Each one contains an "old" strand, and a "new" one.

PAIRING OFF

Each nucleotide in a DNA strand contains one of four bases – adenine (A), thymine (T), cytosine (C), or guanine (G). The chemical structure of the bases means that they can pair up but, as this model illustrates, each can only ever pair with the same partner. Adenine always pairs with thymine. Cytosine always pairs with guanine. These four pairs – AT, TA, CG and GC – make up the "letters" in the DNA code.

UNZIPPING DNA

When DNA copies itself, over 20 different enzymes (p. 7) help to separate the strands and assemble nucleotides in the correct order to make two complementary strands. On average, only one mistake is made for every billion correct duplications of the base-pair sequence. Replication often takes place at many points along the original DNA molecule at the same time, with replication forks unzipping the molecule in opposite directions. Unlike all other substances found in living things, DNA cannot be made without another molecule to act as a template.

New strand

Original strand

Original double helix

Replication fork

Nucleotide

Original strand

New strand

How DNA works

DNA RUNS CELLS BY REMOTE CONTROL. Instead of organizing a cell directly, it instructs the cell to make proteins. These complex and varied chemicals have many different roles. A molecule of DNA can hold the coded plans for thousands of different proteins, and the length of DNA that codes for each of them is known as a gene. Proteins are assembled by linking together chemical units, called amino acids, in an exact order. There are 20 different amino acids, but DNA has to specify them using just four different chemical "letters", or bases (p. 34). So how does it do this? The answer was suggested not by a biologist, but by the astronomer George Gamow, in 1954. He thought DNA might use "words" made up of three letters and, as events proved, his guess was right.

THE MASTER PLAN
A cell's DNA works rather like a set of plans, such as the construction plans for a building project. Some of the cell's plans deal with day-to-day processes that are vital to the cell's well-being, while others deal with processes that may be triggered only once in the cell's lifetime. Rather than being deliberately designed, these plans have been built up over millions of years through the process of evolution (p. 42).

Cell

Nucleus

Chromosome

Histone

Super-coiled DNA

DNA double helix

STORING INFORMATION
In most cells, except those of bacteria, the DNA double helix is coiled around proteins called histones and is located inside the nucleus. The packages of DNA, or chromosomes, cannot be seen, even with an electron microscope, as they are too thin and spread out. However, prior to cell division, the DNA compacts further, or "condenses", by coiling on itself many times. The chromosomes are then visible, at high magnification, as X-shaped bundles of super-coiled DNA.

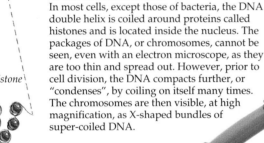

Growing strand of messenger RNA

Template, or sense, strand of DNA

Nucleotide ready for assembly

Non-template strand of DNA

TRANSCRIPTION
The manufacture of a protein is a two-step process. It involves DNA, and also several forms of RNA (p. 34). In the first step, called transcription, part of a DNA strand temporarily unzips. One of the DNA strands acts as a template, and a corresponding strand of messenger RNA, or mRNA, is built up by base-pairing. The single strand of messenger RNA now carries the same information as the DNA strand, although instead of using the base thymine it uses a similar base called uracil. Once an entire gene has been transcribed, the DNA molecule closes up, and the messenger RNA molecule leaves the nucleus of the cell.

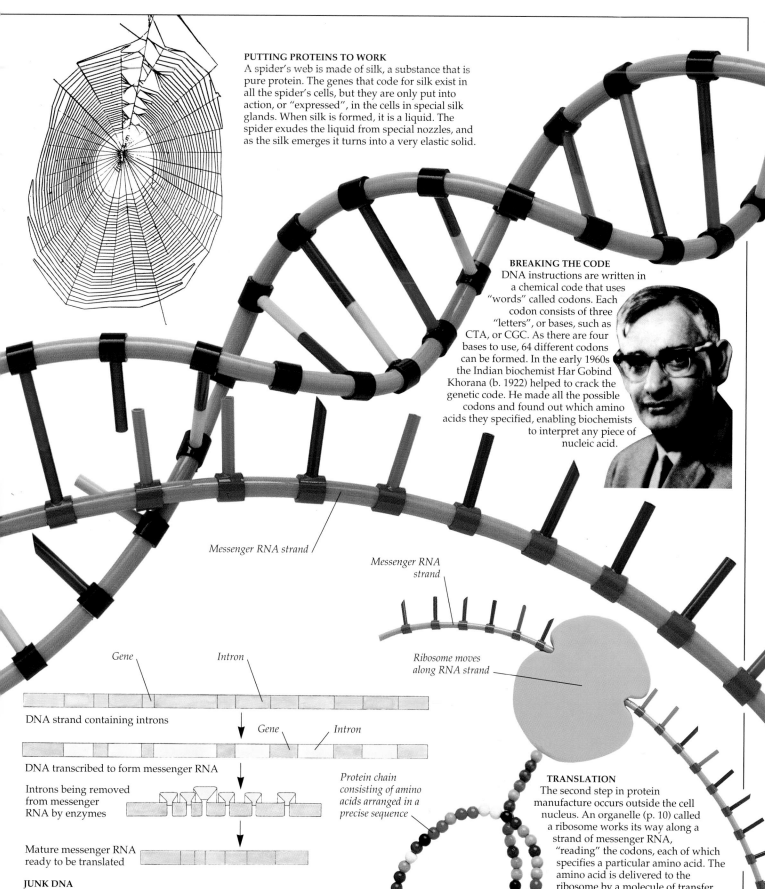

PUTTING PROTEINS TO WORK

A spider's web is made of silk, a substance that is pure protein. The genes that code for silk exist in all the spider's cells, but they are only put into action, or "expressed", in the cells in special silk glands. When silk is formed, it is a liquid. The spider exudes the liquid from special nozzles, and as the silk emerges it turns into a very elastic solid.

BREAKING THE CODE

DNA instructions are written in a chemical code that uses "words" called codons. Each codon consists of three "letters", or bases, such as CTA, or CGC. As there are four bases to use, 64 different codons can be formed. In the early 1960s the Indian biochemist Har Gobind Khorana (b. 1922) helped to crack the genetic code. He made all the possible codons and found out which amino acids they specified, enabling biochemists to interpret any piece of nucleic acid.

Messenger RNA strand

Messenger RNA strand

Ribosome moves along RNA strand

Gene *Intron*

DNA strand containing introns

Gene *Intron*

DNA transcribed to form messenger RNA

Introns being removed from messenger RNA by enzymes

Protein chain consisting of amino acids arranged in a precise sequence

Mature messenger RNA ready to be translated

TRANSLATION

The second step in protein manufacture occurs outside the cell nucleus. An organelle (p. 10) called a ribosome works its way along a strand of messenger RNA, "reading" the codons, each of which specifies a particular amino acid. The amino acid is delivered to the ribosome by a molecule of transfer RNA, or tRNA (not shown here), which slots on to the messenger RNA strand. The amino acid is added to the growing protein chain, the tRNA then disengages, and the ribosome moves on to the next codon. When the ribosome reaches a codon that signals it to stop, the completed protein is released.

JUNK DNA

In the late 1970s biologists discovered that genes are often interrupted by long sequences called introns, which seem to have no meaning. Although the introns are transcribed into RNA, they are removed by enzymes before the RNA is used to make a protein. Some scientists suspect that this "junk" DNA may actually have a hidden role. According to a recent suggestion, introns may form an error-checking system, to ensure that a gene is copied correctly.

Sexual reproduction

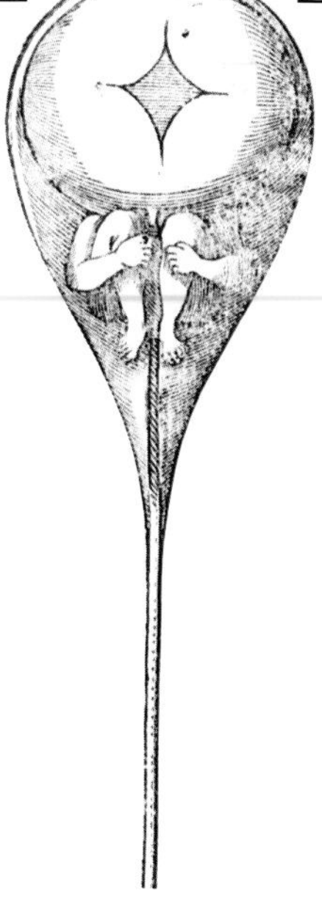

THE EARLIEST FORMS OF LIFE on Earth reproduced without sex. Asexual reproduction (pp. 32-33) can build up numbers very quickly, but it creates no genetic variation. Without variation, a species cannot adapt genetically. In a stable habitat this is not a problem, but if conditions suddenly change, it can prove fatal. At some point in life's history, a new means of reproduction appeared – sexual reproduction, involving two parents instead of one. Each parent produces special sex cells, or gametes, that contain just half the normal number of genes. Sex cells from both parents are brought together and, during a process called fertilization, they join to form one cell. Their genes are combined to create a new individual with its own unique genetic blueprint. This process may sound straightforward, but sexual reproduction actually uses up a great deal of time and resources. The specially formed male and female sex cells must be brought together, and the newly formed cell then needs the right conditions to grow and develop. The fact that sexual reproduction happens at all shows the importance of variation in the living world.

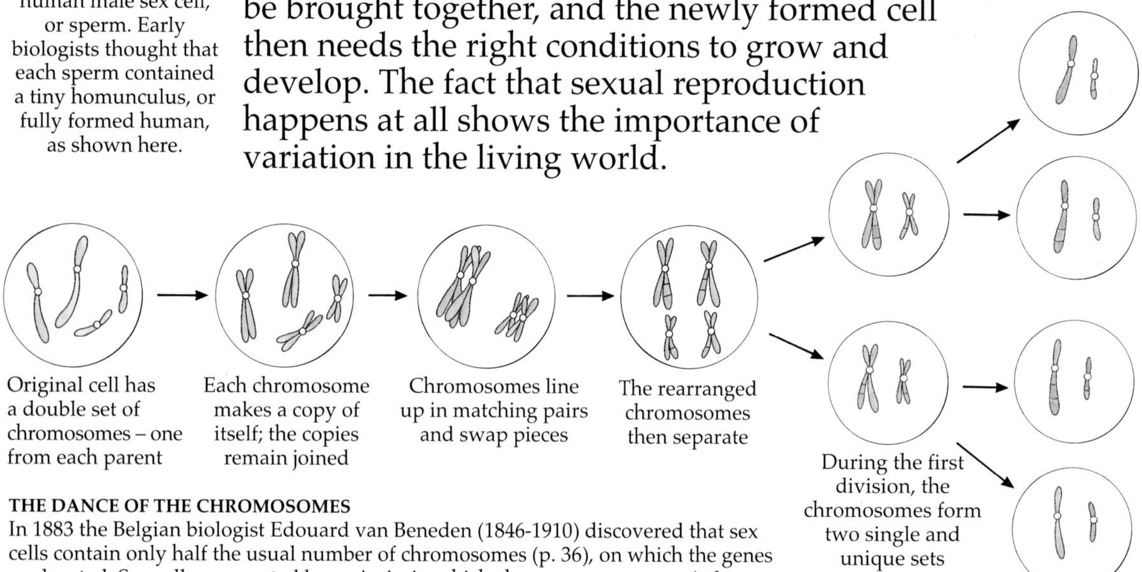

A LIFE IN MINIATURE
This late 17th-century drawing shows a human male sex cell, or sperm. Early biologists thought that each sperm contained a tiny homunculus, or fully formed human, as shown here.

Mature male organs in youngest, highest flowers

Mature female organs in oldest, lowest flowers

Original cell has a double set of chromosomes – one from each parent

Each chromosome makes a copy of itself; the copies remain joined

Chromosomes line up in matching pairs and swap pieces

The rearranged chromosomes then separate

During the first division, the chromosomes form two single and unique sets

During the second division, the arms making up each chromosome separate

THE DANCE OF THE CHROMOSOMES
In 1883 the Belgian biologist Edouard van Beneden (1846-1910) discovered that sex cells contain only half the usual number of chromosomes (p. 36), on which the genes are located. Sex cells are created by meiosis, in which chromosomes are copied once but the cell divides twice. Thus each of the four new cells has just half the number of chromosomes from the original cell. Sex cells also contain unique combinations of genes, because the chromosomes swap pieces before division begins.

SIMILAR BUT DIFFERENT
In myth and folklore, there are many strange tales concerning reproduction. Animals were sometimes thought to give birth to humans, and even in 19th-century England one woman claimed to have given birth to rabbits. However, this kind of reproductive mix-up can never really happen. Offspring always resemble their parents – a pig will always produce piglets, and a sheep will only produce lambs. However, sexual reproduction always creates unique individuals.

SEX IN PLANTS
Most animals are able to move around, so males and females can come together for sexual reproduction. Flowering plants cannot do this, and so they must rely on animals, or on the wind, to carry their male sex cells, or pollen, from one flower to another. Unlike most animals, many flowering plants are hermaphrodites. This means that they have both male and female sex organs, usually in the same flower. In foxglove flowers, male organs mature before female ones. This reduces the chances of self-fertilization and increases the genetic variation of the seeds (p. 39).

BRINGING UP A FAMILY

Sexual reproduction is often a very unequal business. This female *Pholcus* or daddy longlegs spider has put a lot of energy into producing a batch of eggs, and she is holding the eggs in her jaws while they develop. When the spiderlings hatch, the female continues to guard them until they are ready to fend for themselves. The male, meanwhile, is nowhere to be seen. He disappears soon after mating and plays no part in looking after the young.

Ball of eggs held in mother's jaws

Young spiderlings hatching from eggs

RIGHT ON TIME

In sexual reproduction, timing is crucial, because male and female sex cells have to be brought together at exactly the right place and the right moment. The Pacific grunion times its reproduction to fit in with the highest tides of spring. The male and female fish swim close inshore, and are thrown up onto the sand by the waves. The females quickly lay their eggs, and the males fertilize these with their sperm (above). All the fish then return to the water. At the next very high tide the eggs hatch, and the young fish are washed into the sea.

INSIDE A FLOWER

Genetic variation is increased if the sex cells come from two different parents. Like many plants, the foxglove has evolved a way to increase the chances of this happening. Foxglove flowers are pollinated by bumblebees. When a bee that has already visited a foxglove crawls into the lowest flowers, the mature female organs, or stigmas, collect some of the pollen from the bee's back. When the bee reaches the highest flowers, it picks up pollen from their male organs, or anthers, and this is carried off to another plant.

Seeds form in ovary at base of flower

Anthers produce pollen

Bright petals attract bumblebees

Stigma collects pollen

SPAWNING CORAL

This photograph, taken on a reef off Western Australia, shows coral eggs and sperm being released into the sea. The corals all shed their sex cells at exactly the same time, and fertilization occurs in the open water. The fertilized eggs produce tiny larvae that drift far away from their parents.

CAREFUL PARENT

This female leaf beetle is guarding her young family. She produces relatively few young, but by protecting them in early life she increases their chances of survival. Some animals produce very few young and invest considerable time and energy in raising them. Others produce huge numbers of offspring, but do nothing to look after them. A female cod, for example, lays over a million eggs, but nearly all are eaten before they have a chance to grow into adults.

Heredity

IF TWO DIFFERENT-COLOURED PAINTS are mixed, they blend and the original colours cannot be separated. When two organisms breed by sexual reproduction, some characteristics do seem to blend, but others often vanish, only to reappear in later generations. To the Austrian monk Gregor Johann Mendel (1822–1884), this suggested that heredity – the link between generations – must obey some system of rules. In the monastery gardens, Mendel carried out experiments on the common garden pea. By carefully controlling which plant bred with which, he recorded how characteristics such as flower colour were passed on. Mendel concluded that inherited characteristics do not blend, but remain separate. Each characteristic is determined by two factors, or "elements", one from each parent. Of each pair of factors, one is often "dominant", meaning that it masks the other. However, the masked or "recessive" factor does not disappear, and it may become unmasked in later generations. Although Mendel's work was published in 1865, it was not until the 20th century that its true importance was finally appreciated.

GENES AND THE ENVIRONMENT
Kittens are produced by sexual reproduction, so each has a unique genetic blueprint, or genotype. However, only some of its alleles will actually be put into action, or expressed. The kitten's physical being, or phenotype, is the product of its genotype and the conditions in which it lives.

ACTING TOGETHER
During his experiments, Mendel examined characteristics that were controlled by alleles of a single gene. However, heredity is not always this straightforward. For example, the shape of the comb on a cockerel's head is controlled by alleles not of one gene but of two complementary genes. On their own, the alleles of each gene produce small flattened combs. If they are inherited together, as often happens, they can produce the tall comb seen on this bird.

POLYGENIC INHERITANCE
Human eye colour is controlled principally by one gene. One allele of this gene produces brown eyes, and another produces blue. However, eye colour can also be affected by "modifier" genes, which alter the actual colour that is produced. Different combinations of modifier genes produce colours such as hazel, green, and grey. This is known as polygenic inheritance, and it explains why some characteristics seem to blend.

Blue eyes – two recessive alleles, no modifier genes

Brown eyes – two dominant alleles, no modifier genes

Hazel eyes – modifier genes alter the amount and distribution of pigment in the eye

Green eyes – created by the presence of modifier genes

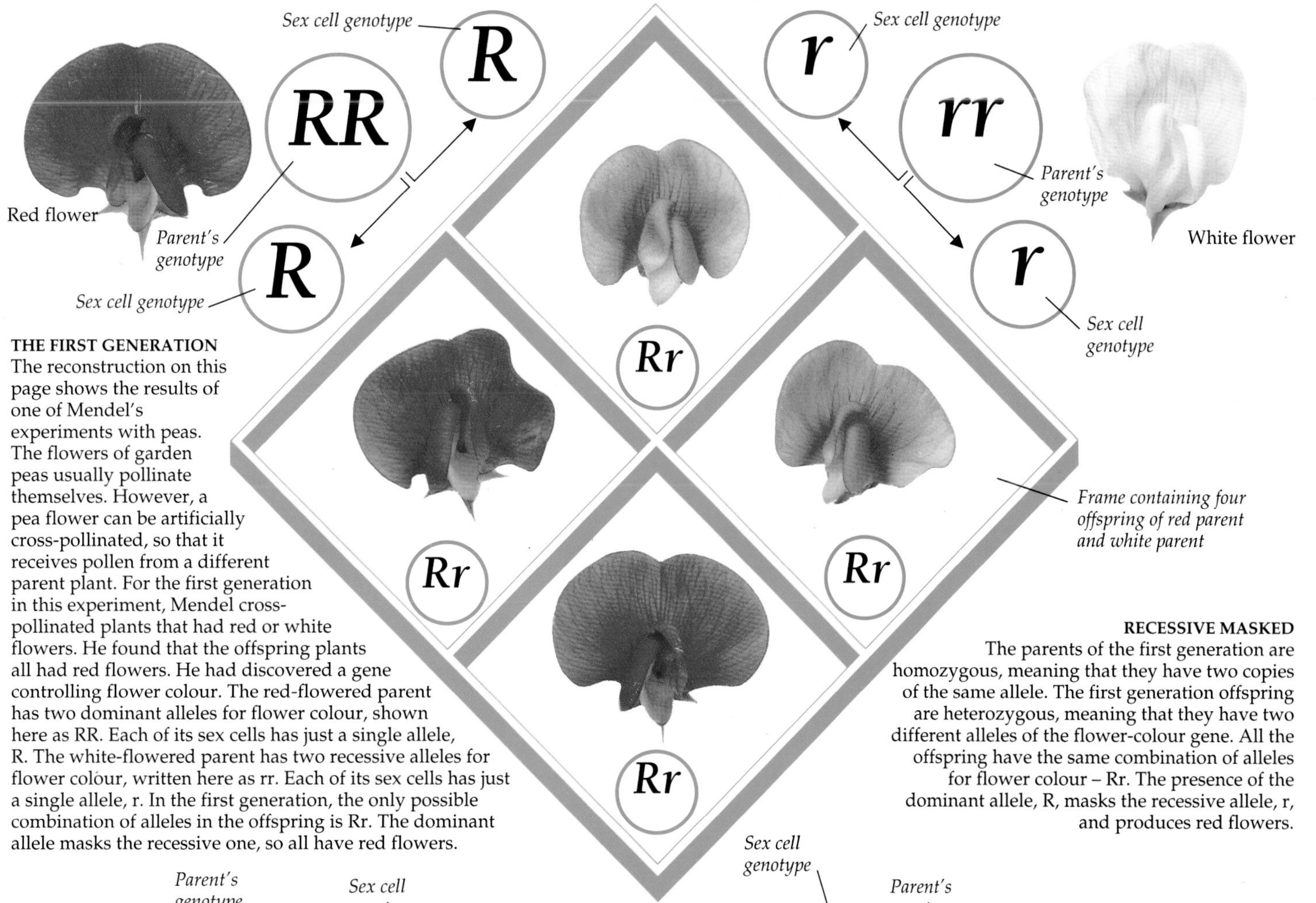

Sex cell genotype — **R**

RR
Red flower

Parent's genotype

Sex cell genotype — **R**

THE FIRST GENERATION
The reconstruction on this page shows the results of one of Mendel's experiments with peas. The flowers of garden peas usually pollinate themselves. However, a pea flower can be artificially cross-pollinated, so that it receives pollen from a different parent plant. For the first generation in this experiment, Mendel cross-pollinated plants that had red or white flowers. He found that the offspring plants all had red flowers. He had discovered a gene controlling flower colour. The red-flowered parent has two dominant alleles for flower colour, shown here as RR. Each of its sex cells has just a single allele, R. The white-flowered parent has two recessive alleles for flower colour, written here as rr. Each of its sex cells has just a single allele, r. In the first generation, the only possible combination of alleles in the offspring is Rr. The dominant allele masks the recessive one, so all have red flowers.

Sex cell genotype — **r**

rr
Parent's genotype

White flower

r — *Sex cell genotype*

Rr **Rr** **Rr** **Rr**

Frame containing four offspring of red parent and white parent

RECESSIVE MASKED
The parents of the first generation are homozygous, meaning that they have two copies of the same allele. The first generation offspring are heterozygous, meaning that they have two different alleles of the flower-colour gene. All the offspring have the same combination of alleles for flower colour – Rr. The presence of the dominant allele, R, masks the recessive allele, r, and produces red flowers.

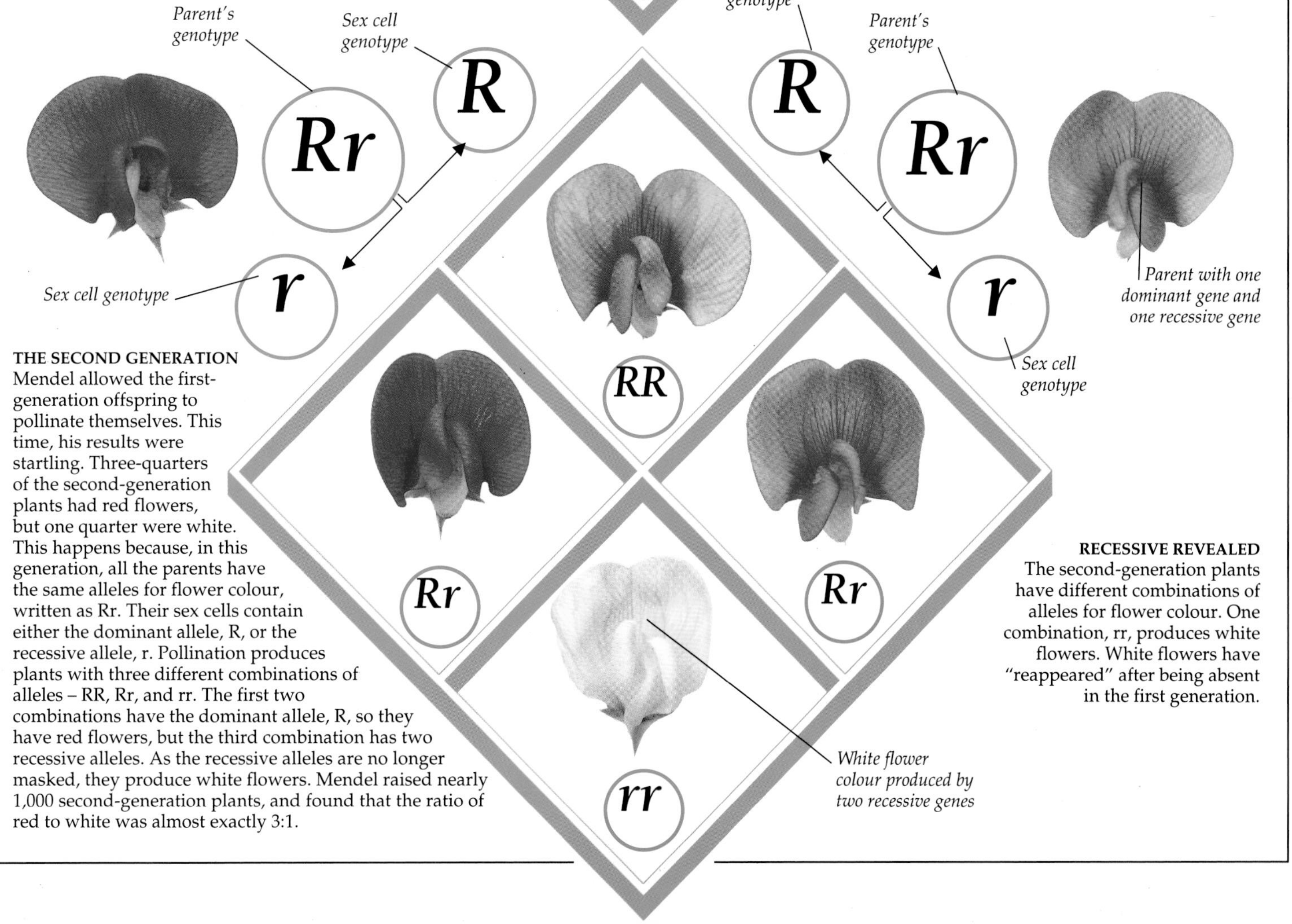

Parent's genotype *Sex cell genotype* — **R**

Rr

Sex cell genotype — **r**

THE SECOND GENERATION
Mendel allowed the first-generation offspring to pollinate themselves. This time, his results were startling. Three-quarters of the second-generation plants had red flowers, but one quarter were white. This happens because, in this generation, all the parents have the same alleles for flower colour, written as Rr. Their sex cells contain either the dominant allele, R, or the recessive allele, r. Pollination produces plants with three different combinations of alleles – RR, Rr, and rr. The first two combinations have the dominant allele, R, so they have red flowers, but the third combination has two recessive alleles. As the recessive alleles are no longer masked, they produce white flowers. Mendel raised nearly 1,000 second-generation plants, and found that the ratio of red to white was almost exactly 3:1.

Sex cell genotype — **R**

Parent's genotype

Rr

r — *Sex cell genotype*

Parent with one dominant gene and one recessive gene

RR **Rr** **Rr** **rr**

RECESSIVE REVEALED
The second-generation plants have different combinations of alleles for flower colour. One combination, rr, produces white flowers. White flowers have "reappeared" after being absent in the first generation.

White flower colour produced by two recessive genes

Evolution

IN THE NATURAL WORLD, like only breeds with like. A group of living things that can breed together is known as a species. Until the late 17th century it was thought that each species had been individually designed and created for a particular purpose, but new knowledge threw doubt on this idea. Geological evidence showed that the Earth was far older than was once thought. Fossils showed that many ancient forms of life had vanished and that species seemed to change, or evolve, over time. In the 19th century two British naturalists, Charles Darwin (1809-1882) and Alfred Russel Wallace (1823-1913), proposed a cause for this evolution – the weeding out of inherited variations, favouring some members of a species at the expense of others. This process of "natural selection" forms a key part of modern biology.

STRUGGLING TO SURVIVE
Female butterflies lay hundreds of eggs. If all of these became adults, butterflies would swamp the surface of the Earth, but this never happens because the caterpillars face a struggle to survive – avoiding being eaten and competing with their kin.

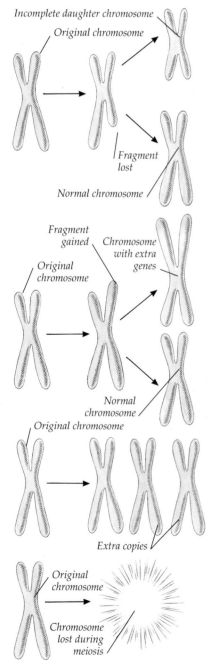

Incomplete daughter chromosome

Original chromosome

Fragment lost

Normal chromosome

Fragment gained

Chromosome with extra genes

Original chromosome

Normal chromosome

Original chromosome

Extra copies

Original chromosome

Chromosome lost during meiosis

THE ORIGIN OF VARIATION
Variation in a species is caused by accidental changes in the chemical sequence held by DNA (p. 34). These changes are called mutations. If the mutation is present in a sex cell or gamete, it may be handed on to future generations. Most mutations result from errors when a DNA molecule replicates itself (p. 35). Others occur when entire chromosomes are altered in some way. Here a chromosome has lost a fragment of one arm. After cell division, each half becomes a new chromosome. One is the same as the original, but the other is missing a number of genes.

GAINING GENES
If a cell is exposed to a "mutagenic agent", such as ultraviolet light, its chromosomes may break and one can gain a fragment from another. After cell division, one new chromosome has the same genes as the original, but the other has the extra genes added on.

CHANGING NUMBERS
Occasionally, more than one copy of a chromosome is made, resulting in a cell that has extra copies of a particular chromosome. Sometimes the result is a polyploid cell, or one that has multiple copies of all its chromosomes. Polyploidy is common in plants.

LOSING CHROMOSOMES
During meiosis (p. 38), sex cells or gametes sometimes end up with less than a full single set of chromosomes. After fertilization, they produce offspring that do not have a complete double set of genes. Mutations like this are rarely handed on, because they usually result in sterility.

SEXUAL SELECTION

Natural selection is not the only force that can create change. Darwin realized that change could also be produced by sexual selection. This occurs in species where one sex – usually the female – chooses its mate. They may choose the strongest males, or those with the best territories. When these differences are genetic, this selection results – after many generations – in a change in the gene pool. Female pheasants, for example, often choose males with the brightest plumage, resulting in males with brilliant colours, like this one.

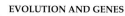

THE LOTTERY OF LIFE

Caterpillars are produced by sexual reproduction (p. 38), so each has a slightly different collection of genes and therefore a different collection of characteristics. Some are able to eat more quickly than their siblings, while others are better at digesting their food or at avoiding their enemies. A few are quicker to set off in search of new sources of food when their existing food begins to run out. The environment is a proving ground for each collection of genes. The caterpillars with the most suitable characteristics will survive to reproduce, so they will pass on their genes to future generations. Those with unsuitable characteristics will die without reproducing. As this process is repeated generation after generation, the species will slowly change, so that it becomes genetically better adapted to its way of life.

ASSEMBLING THE EVIDENCE

Charles Darwin spent over 20 years gathering evidence to support his ideas on evolution and natural selection. He finally published his findings in 1859, in one of the most famous books in science, *The Origin of Species*.

Caterpillar moving away in search of new food source

ARTIFICIAL SELECTION

Cultivated bananas are far bigger than those that grow in the wild. Most varieties are also sterile, which means that they can only be propagated by taking cuttings. Like most crops, cultivated bananas have been produced by artificial selection. Farmers and growers have consistently favoured particular characteristics, so that new kinds of plant have gradually emerged. Charles Darwin used artificial selection as evidence to show that species were capable of change.

EVOLUTION AND GENES

Darwin knew nothing about genetics (p. 40), and he believed that inherited characteristics blended, instead of being kept separate. However, his ideas about natural selection are quite easily explained by looking at genes. The diagrams below show the frequency of two alleles, or forms of the same gene, in an imaginary population of animals. As time goes by, natural selection favours one allele at the expense of the other. The result is a gradual change in the pool of genes – in other words, evolution.

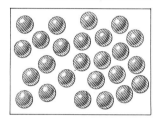

To start with, most animals have the green allele.

Animals with the yellow allele consistently have more young.

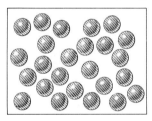

As yellow alleles increase, the green alleles decrease.

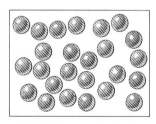

By this stage, most animals have the yellow allele.

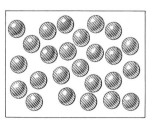

The overall gene pool has altered, so the species can be said to have evolved.

Interactions within species

AN ANIMAL'S GENETIC BLUEPRINT is not just a construction plan. As well as containing instructions for physical characteristics such as brown feathers, sharp teeth, or wrinkly skin, it also contains instructions for behaviour. Behaviour is whatever an animal does, and how it does it. It consists of different actions that help an animal to survive and to reproduce. Even simple organisms, such as single-celled Paramecium (p. 13), can have quite complex behaviour. *Paramecium* normally backs away from obstacles and then changes course. To carry out sexual reproduction, however, it has to line up with a partner. Although *Paramecium* does not have a nervous system or any sense organs, it can tell the difference between a partner and an obstacle, and it then behaves in an appropriate way. In more complex animals, interactions between members of the same species are much more elaborate. Most animals have ways of communicating with rivals or relatives, and many have special courtship rituals that they use to acquire a mate. Some animals have evolved special ways of life that depend on working together. Among insects, these "social" lifestyles reach a peak in the world of ants, bees, and wasps. The ability to cooperate "socially" is one of the reasons why these animals are so successful and so widespread.

LEARNING TO BEHAVE
In most animals, some kinds of behaviour are inherited, and some are learned. This young kangaroo was born with an in-built behaviour pattern, or instinct, that made it climb into its mother's pouch. As it grows up, it will learn other kinds of behaviour by watching its mother. These will include how to find food, how to react to other kangaroos, and how to respond to danger.

Dancing bee

Worker bees feel the movements of a fellow worker dancing on the honeycomb and directing them towards nectar

PASSING ON INFORMATION
In summer, a honeybee hive is the scene of hectic activity. Streams of worker bees forage for food, and return laden with nectar and pollen. Some bees stand guard at the entrance while others fan their wings to keep the hive cool. On the sloping honeycomb inside the dark hive, foraging bees use a special "waggle dance" to tell other bees how far away food is, and in what direction to go. A bee moves in a circle, which it then crosses. The angle at which it crosses the circle, relative to gravity, tells the others the direction of the food relative to the Sun, and the smaller the circle, the nearer the food.

Path of waggle dance

Worker ant with piece of leaf following scent trail to nest

TRACING A MESSAGE
Animals communicate in many different ways. This male moth has large feathery antennae that can detect tiny amounts of an airborne chemical called a pheromone. This is given off by the female to attract a mate.

Antennae

LIVING TOGETHER
Like all ants, leafcutter ants always live in family groups, or colonies. Each colony consists of a queen ant – the only one to lay eggs – and her offspring. These can number tens of thousands. The larger offspring, called soldiers, defend the nest, while the smaller offspring, called workers, slice off pieces of leaves and carry them underground. Here, the leaves are used to grow a fungus that the ants eat. How has this kind of behaviour evolved? Why have soldiers and workers "given up" reproducing, when reproduction is the main function of all living things? During the second half of this century, the American biologist E. O. Wilson (b. 1929) has set about trying to answer these questions. He and others have developed an entirely new science called sociobiology.

Robin

Ant slicing
off piece of leaf

Map of robin territories

2 1

House

Road

3

4 5

6

7

Individual
territories

Antennae used to
identify scent of
other ants

ISSUING A CHALLENGE

Why do robins sing?
The answer is not to please
us, or to pass the time of day.
Instead, a robin's song is a
warning and a challenge. It tells
other robins that it has claimed a
territory, and says that rival robins enter
at their peril. By setting up a territory, a
robin guarantees itself a supply of food, and this
gives it the best chance of raising a family. The map
above, based on research by the British
ornithologist David Lack, shows seven
robin territories surrounding a house.
Like all territories, their boundaries
change as time goes by.

FINDING A LEVEL

In animal societies,
members compete to be in
control. Eventually, they
establish an order of
dominance called a
hierarchy. Monkeys and
other primates often live in
groups, and their
hierarchies are expressed in
grooming. When two
monkeys meet, the dominant
one is always first groomed by
one that is lower down in the
hierarchy. The dominant monkey
then returns the favour.

Subordinate
animal

STUDYING BEHAVIOUR

The Austrian biologist Konrad
Lorenz (1903–1989)
helped to found
ethology, or the
modern science of
behaviour. He
believed that most
kinds of behaviour
are inherited. In one
famous study, he
showed that young
birds "lock on" to
their parents by a
special kind of
learning that he
called imprinting.
He believed that
this ability has a
genetic basis.

Dominant
animal

Interactions between species

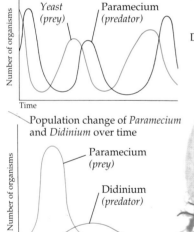

EVOLVING TOGETHER

To make seeds, flowering plants usually have to transfer pollen (p. 38). Many of them do this by attracting insect visitors, such as bees. A bee visits flowers to feed on their pollen and nectar, and in return it carries pollen from one flower to another.

This is an example of a kind of partnership called mutualism, in which both species stand to gain. It seems like a deliberate arrangement but, as always in evolution, it has come about through a series of random chances, and the partnership is not always a "fair" one. Some plants cheat their insect visitors by failing to provide nectar, and some bees cut holes in flowers so that they can reach the nectar more easily. They get their meal, but do not transfer any pollen.

JUST AFTER MIDDAY on September 1, 1914, a bird called Martha died in a zoo in Cincinatti, Ohio, in the USA. She was 29 years old and she was the last remaining passenger pigeon on Earth. At the beginning of the 1800s, there were probably 10 thousand million of her kind in North America, making passenger pigeons the most numerous birds on Earth. But their gigantic flocks were easy targets, and in the century that followed, hunters simply blasted the pigeons out of the sky or out of their tree-top roosts. The slaughter was so rapid and so widespread that the species never recovered. The passenger pigeon's story is an unusual and very extreme example of an interaction between one species and another. In nature, all forms of life are involved in a struggle for survival, but complicated balances have evolved, so there are rarely outright "winners" or "losers" like the passenger pigeon. A lion that kills an antelope, or a shrew that kills an earthworm, is certainly the winner of that particular contest, but lions never kill all antelopes, just as shrews never kill all earthworms. If they did, they themselves would soon become extinct for lack of food. Different species not only interact as predators or prey; many have evolved special partnerships, called symbioses, in which two species live closely together. Sometimes both species benefit, but often the alliance is onesided, with one partner getting more out of it than the other. In nature, there is no such thing as fair play. Each partner grabs as much as possible to ensure its survival.

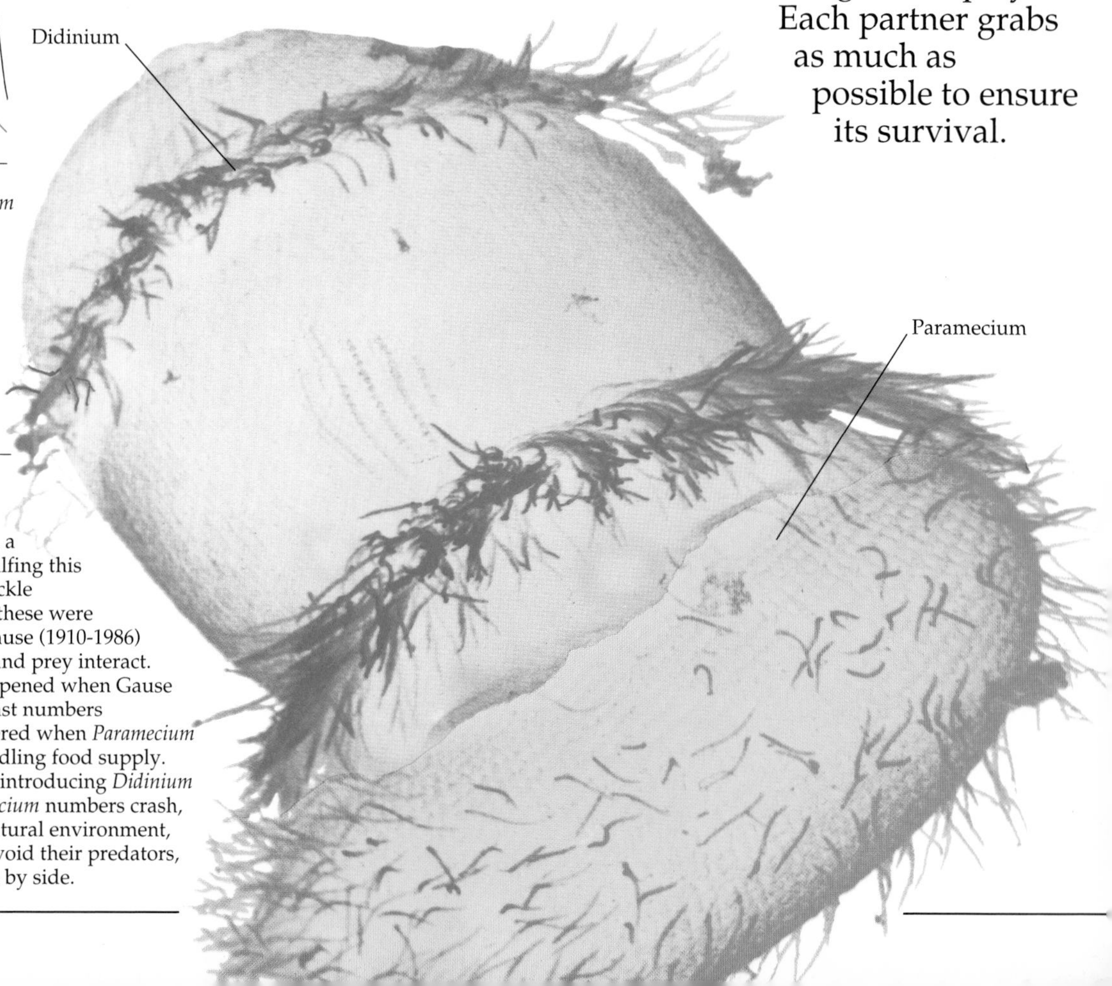

Population change of yeast and *Paramecium* over time

Yeast (prey) Paramecium (predator)

Number of organisms

Time

Population change of *Paramecium* and *Didinium* over time

Paramecium (prey)

Didinium (predator)

Number of organisms

Time

Didinium

Paramecium

PREDATOR AND PREY

In this battle to the death (right), a microscopic *Didinium* attacks its prey, a *Paramecium*. Just two hours after engulfing this meal, the *Didinium* will be ready to tackle another. Single-celled organisms like these were used by the Russian ecologist G. F. Gause (1910-1986) to investigate exactly how predators and prey interact. The top graph above shows what happened when Gause kept *Paramecium* with a yeast. The yeast numbers periodically dropped, but then recovered when *Paramecium* levels dropped as a result of the dwindling food supply. The bottom graph shows the effect of introducing *Didinium* into a tank of *Paramecium*. The *Paramecium* numbers crash, and both species die out. In a more natural environment, some *Paramecium* would manage to avoid their predators, so the two species would survive side by side.

UNWILLING HOST

Parasitism is the most unequal of nature's partnerships. A parasite lives at the expense of another organism – called its host. The spaghetti-like strands hanging on this tree are stems of dodder, a parasitic plant. The dodder stems force their way into their host's cells, and rob them of nutrients and water.

UNHAPPY LANDING

Most plants get all the minerals that they need from the soil, but in swampy places minerals are often hard to come by. The Venus flytrap has evolved its own answer to this problem. It has special hinged leaves, which snap shut if insects land on them. The plant digests its victims, and uses the minerals that their bodies contain. Once an insect has been digested, the leaves open and the deadly trap is set once more.

Trapped dragonfly

Interlocking spikes

Leaves of Venus flytrap

Hinge

CASHING IN

As the crew of a fishing boat hauls in nets filled with fish, a flock of gulls descends, intent on its share of the catch. Together, gulls and humans form a commensal partnership – a partnership in which one species gains, but the other neither benefits nor suffers harm. Commensalism is quite difficult to prove in nature. This is because it is hard to be sure that one partner is not actually harming the other.

A PLACE IN THE SUN

All plants need light in order to grow. Some low-growing plants get their share of the light by perching on the branches of trees and shrubs. These plants are called epiphytes. They include air plants, like this one, as well as many ferns and mosses. Unlike parasitic plants, such as dodder, epiphytes do not take any nutrients from their hosts.

EATER AND EATEN

A shrew is a highly active mammal, and its body burns up food at a very rapid rate. To stay alive, it needs an almost non-stop supply of earthworms, insects and other small animals. However, as the shrew scurries about in search of food, it puts itself in danger, because its own predators are always waiting to pounce. Many animals reduce the risk to themselves by lying in wait for their prey. Although this method of hunting results in a smaller catch, there is less chance of falling prey to another predator.

Shrew

Earthworm

Classifying living things

AT LEAST TWO MILLION DIFFERENT KINDS OF LIVING THINGS are known to science, and many more are added to the list every year. Some of these organisms are very familiar, and their names are well-known. Others have no common names at all, either because they live in places where humans rarely go, or because they are small or inconspicuous and are easily overlooked. However, in biology, every form of life is important. To make sense of the living world, biologists must be able to identify different organisms in a way that ensures that one form is never confused with another. To do this, they rely on a system devised by the Swedish botanist Carl von Linné, also known as Carolus Linnaeus (1707-1778). He gave a unique two-part name, or binomial, to each species that he described. The second part of the binomial identifies the species, while the first part shows which other species are its close relatives. By classifying species in groups of increasing size, biologists can show how different life forms are thought to be linked by evolution.

A PASSION FOR ORDER
Linnaeus was a tireless and observant worker. He set out to describe and name all the forms of life then known, using his own binomial classification system. He did not believe in evolution, but his system is now used to indicate relationships between species.

The library of life

Biological classification works like the filing system in a library. Like books, species are classified in increasingly large groupings. A genus is like an individual shelf containing a row of books on closely related subjects, whilst a family is like a stack of shelves. An order is like a single bookcase, and a class is a row of bookcases in one area. The system continues until it reaches the highest level, a kingdom, which is like a whole library floor. As in a real library, species can be moved or reclassified as ideas change about the way they are related. The animals below show how the system works, taking a species of beetle as an example.

NAME THAT PLANT
A 12th-century book shows a European wild gladiolus and defines it by its medicinal "virtues" or uses. As scholars discovered more plants, the names became ever longer. Linnaeus devised a simple two-part name for each one, and this now forms the basis of scientific classification.

Sternotomis vulgaris

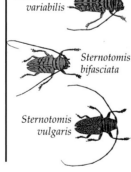

Sternotomis variabilis

Sternotomis bifasciata

Sternotomis vulgaris

Monochamus ruspator

Clytus sp.

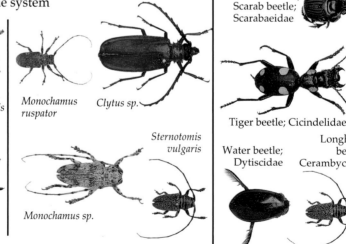

Sternotomis vulgaris

Monochamus sp.

Scarab beetle; Scarabaeidae

Tiger beetle; Cicindelidae

Water beetle; Dytiscidae

Longhorn beetle; Cerambycidae

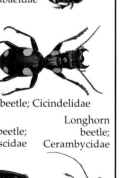

Cicada; order Hemiptera

Dragonfly; order Odonata

SPECIES
Sternotomis vulgaris is the scientific name, or binomial, that identifies one particular species of longhorn beetle. The second part of the binomial, *vulgaris*, distinguishes this species from its close relatives in the genus *Sternotomis*. *Vulgaris* is Latin for "common", and many species have this as the second part of their binomial.

GENUS *STERNOTOMIS*
All these beetles are members of the same genus (plural genera), a collection of closely related species. All the species share the same generic name, in this case *Sternotomis*. When species in the same genus are being compared, the generic name is often abbreviated to become, for example, *S. vulgaris*.

FAMILY CERAMBYCIDAE
The genus *Sternotomis* is one of several that are included in the family Cerambycidae, or longhorn beetles. The members of this family all have very long antennae. Their larvae often bore their way through trees, and can take several years to become adult. The entire family contains over 20,000 species, including some that are serious pests of timber.

ORDER COLEOPTERA
The longhorned beetles belong to the order Coleoptera, which contains all the world's beetles – at least 350,000 species. Beetles have two pairs of wings. Their forewings have evolved to form hard, curved cases called elytra which meet in a line down the back of the body.

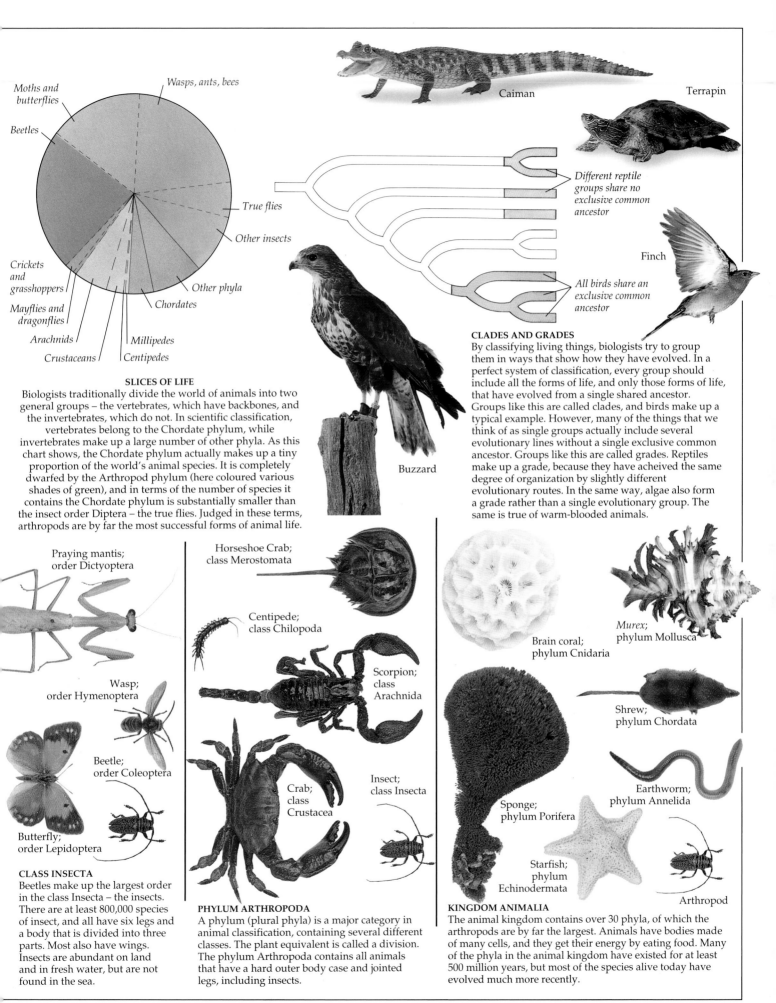

Moths and butterflies

Beetles

Wasps, ants, bees

True flies

Other insects

Crickets and grasshoppers

Other phyla

Chordates

Mayflies and dragonflies

Arachnids

Crustaceans

Millipedes

Centipedes

Caiman

Terrapin

Different reptile groups share no exclusive common ancestor

Finch

All birds share an exclusive common ancestor

Buzzard

SLICES OF LIFE
Biologists traditionally divide the world of animals into two general groups – the vertebrates, which have backbones, and the invertebrates, which do not. In scientific classification, vertebrates belong to the Chordate phylum, while invertebrates make up a large number of other phyla. As this chart shows, the Chordate phylum actually makes up a tiny proportion of the world's animal species. It is completely dwarfed by the Arthropod phylum (here coloured various shades of green), and in terms of the number of species it contains the Chordate phylum is substantially smaller than the insect order Diptera – the true flies. Judged in these terms, arthropods are by far the most successful forms of animal life.

CLADES AND GRADES
By classifying living things, biologists try to group them in ways that show how they have evolved. In a perfect system of classification, every group should include all the forms of life, and only those forms of life, that have evolved from a single shared ancestor. Groups like this are called clades, and birds make up a typical example. However, many of the things that we think of as single groups actually include several evolutionary lines without a single exclusive common ancestor. Groups like this are called grades. Reptiles make up a grade, because they have acheived the same degree of organization by slightly different evolutionary routes. In the same way, algae also form a grade rather than a single evolutionary group. The same is true of warm-blooded animals.

Praying mantis; order Dictyoptera

Horseshoe Crab; class Merostomata

Centipede; class Chilopoda

Brain coral; phylum Cnidaria

Murex; phylum Mollusca

Wasp; order Hymenoptera

Scorpion; class Arachnida

Beetle; order Coleoptera

Crab; class Crustacea

Insect; class Insecta

Shrew; phylum Chordata

Butterfly; order Lepidoptera

Sponge; phylum Porifera

Earthworm; phylum Annelida

Starfish; phylum Echinodermata

Arthropod

CLASS INSECTA
Beetles make up the largest order in the class Insecta – the insects. There are at least 800,000 species of insect, and all have six legs and a body that is divided into three parts. Most also have wings. Insects are abundant on land and in fresh water, but are not found in the sea.

PHYLUM ARTHROPODA
A phylum (plural phyla) is a major category in animal classification, containing several different classes. The plant equivalent is called a division. The phylum Arthropoda contains all animals that have a hard outer body case and jointed legs, including insects.

KINGDOM ANIMALIA
The animal kingdom contains over 30 phyla, of which the arthropods are by far the largest. Animals have bodies made of many cells, and they get their energy by eating food. Many of the phyla in the animal kingdom have existed for at least 500 million years, but most of the species alive today have evolved much more recently.

Kingdoms of life

W HEN LINNAEUS CLASSIFIED LIVING THINGS (p. 48), he used two overall divisions of nature – plants and animals. As biologists began to look more closely at living things, particularly those that could only be seen with a microscope, it became clear that this neat distinction did not always work. Some single-celled forms of life seemed to be like both plants and animals, while others were like neither. Today, biologists use several more kingdoms in their classification of life. One commonly accepted system divides the whole of life into five kingdoms. The Kingdom Monera contains the bacteria. The Kingdom Protista contains a very varied collection of mainly single-celled organisms, while the Kingdom Fungi contains mostly multicellular organisms that absorb food from their surroundings. The multicellular organisms of the Plant and Animal Kingdoms live in very different ways.

MYSTERIOUS FUNGI
For a long time, fungi were not considered to be living things at all. Even when people realized that fungi were alive, their exact nature remained a mystery. They seemed to grow like plants, but had no roots or leaves, and produced no seeds. Today, fungi are classified in a kingdom of their own, but they still appear in botanical textbooks and are often described as plants.

Monera

Monerans are organisms with a single prokaryotic cell – a cell that does not contain a nucleus or any membrane-bound organelles. Monerans include bacteria and cyanobacteria (once known as blue-green algae). Monerans are the simplest life forms in existence and they normally reproduce by binary fission (p. 32). For more than 2 million million years they were the only forms of life on Earth. Today they are still abundant and they play an important role in recycling mineral nutrients. The kingdom contains at least 4,000 species.

CONJUGATION
These *Escherichia coli* bacteria (below) are exchanging genes in a process called conjugation. Two or more bacteria connect together with tiny threads. Small loops of DNA, called plasmids (p. 61), then move along the threads from the donor bacterium to the recipient.

GLIDING BACTERIA
Oscillatoria is a common cyanobacterium that grows in water and always reproduces asexually. Its cells form long jelly-covered filaments. Cyanobacteria make food by photosynthesis (p. 16). Some glide along by a mechanism that is not yet understood.

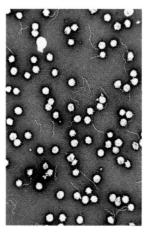

BACTERIA AND DISEASE
These spiral bacteria, seen among blood cells, are *Borellia recurrens* – the cause of a disease called relapsing fever. Despite their bad reputation, most bacteria are either beneficial or harmless.

SLIME MOULDS
Despite their name, slime moulds are usually classified as protists, not fungi. Cellular slime moulds consist of separate independent cells that join together to reproduce (p. 15).

Protista

Protists are organisms with a single eukaryotic cell – a cell that contains a nucleus and membrane-bound organelles. Protists are extremely varied, and are much larger and more complex than monerans. Some make their food by photosynthesis (p.16). Others behave more like animals, and collect food from their surroundings. Some biologists include all algae in this kingdom, even those with more than one cell. There are at least 50,000 protist species.

ON THE MOVE
Protozoa are animal-like protists that move about to find food. These ciliates move about by beating large numbers of tiny hairs, or cilia. Other protozoa have longer threads, called flagella, or move by changing their shape (p. 13).

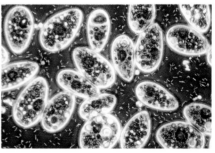

LIVING IN A GLASS SCULPTURE
Much of the ocean floor is covered by a thick layer of ooze. It consists of billions of tiny sculpted cases, made from silica by protists called radiolarians. This is an electron micrograph of a single radiolarian skeleton. The outer part is broken open, revealing the interior. The living radiolarian has thread-like pseudopods (p. 13) that extend around the case to collect food.

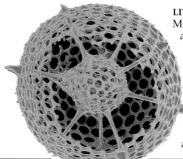

Fungi

Although some fungi look like plants, they cannot make food by photosynthesis (p. 16). Recent research suggests that they may even be more closely related to animals than to plants. Most fungi absorb organic matter from their surroundings through slender threads called hyphae. Many fungi live on dead matter, but some invade living organisms. Fungi often become visible only when they produce the fruiting bodies that make "seed" packets called spores. Some fungi catapult their spores away. Others simply shed them into the wind or disperse them by attracting animal visitors. This kingdom probably contains at least 100,000 species.

LURING FLIES

Clathrus archeri (right) is an extraordinary Australasian fungus with bright red arms that look like tentacles. It grows on the ground in pastures or woodland and attracts flies with its powerful and sickening smell. The flies settle on the sticky spores and then carry them away. By doing this, they help the fungus to spread.

GILLED FUNGUS

A toadstool is a large fruiting body made of a mass of tiny threads, or hyphae. When it is mature, pores or gills under the toadstool's cap shed millions of spores into the surrounding air. The spores are so light that they can be carried high into the atmosphere. This woodland species is *Lepiota aspersa*.

SPORES ON STALKS

Fungi that produce mushrooms and toadstools are members of a large group called the basidiomycetes. They produce their spores from microscopic club-shaped structures called basidia. Each basidium forms four spores that are attached to it by slender stalks.

GROWING FROM AN EGG

The fruiting body of the dog stinkhorn starts as a white, egg-shaped object partly buried below ground. When the "egg" is ripe, its top splits open and a hollow shaft rapidly grows upwards. At the top is a slimy and putrid-smelling mass of spores that quickly attracts visiting flies. Within a few hours, most of the spores have been dispersed, glued to the flies' legs.

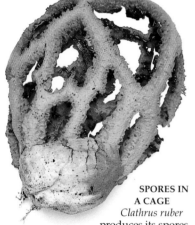

SPORES IN A CAGE

Clathrus ruber produces its spores on the inside of an open, rounded cage. Like its relatives, it attracts insect visitors to its spores by producing a powerful smell. As with other fungi, the fruiting body grows from long fine threads that feed on organic matter. These break if the fruiting body is pulled up, which is why fungi seem to have no "roots".

LIVING ON THE BODY

Candida albicans is a microscopic fungus that is rather like yeast (p. 32). It grows on body surfaces but is usually kept in check by bacteria, so it does no harm. However, if the bacteria die back – for example, as the result of treatment by antibiotics – the fungus can grow quickly and spread.

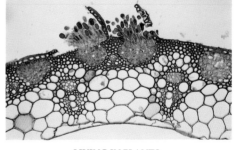

LIVING IN PLANTS

Puccinia graminis is one of many tiny fungi that live in plants and cause diseases called rusts. In this micro-photograph, fungal threads are forcing their way out of a leaf to release spores.

BREAD MOULD

If a piece of bread is left in a damp place, it turns mouldy. Mould consists of fungal threads that spread through organic matter. This slice of bread is providing food for several different moulds. Each colony has been produced by a single spore.

SHOOTING SPORES

This scarlet elf cup (left) belongs to the largest group of fungi, which are known as the ascomycetes. These fungi produce their spores in microscopic cylindrical sacs called asci. When the spores are ripe, the top of the ascus breaks open and the spores shoot out, often at considerable speed. The scarlet elf cup (*Sarcoscypha coccinea*) lives on dead wood.

DESTROYERS AND RECYCLERS

Bisporella citrina belongs to a family of fungi that usually lives on dead matter, such as wood, or on living plants, absorbing nutrients through their hyphae. Fungi are essential recyclers of nutrients, so they are of great value to plants, but they can also kill their living hosts. Many trees die from severe fungal infection.

Plants and animals

PLANTS AND ANIMALS ARE NOT the oldest forms of life on Earth, but in terms of the numbers of species they are by far the most abundant. The members of both kingdoms are made of many cells, but they live in very different ways. Plants make food from simple materials by photosynthesis (p. 16). Animals cannot do this; they must take in their food ready-made. Despite cataloguing life for over 200 years, biologists still have no exact idea how many species of plants and animals exist. Botanists are sure that there are about 550 species of conifer on Earth, but small animals are much harder to track down and to tell apart. About 15,000 species of nematode worms have been classified, but some zoologists think that there may be 500,000.

BURSTING AT THE SEAMS
According to the Bible, Noah loaded up his ark with a male and female of every animal species on Earth. Over one million species of animal have now been identified by scientists, so Noah's ark would have been well laden with its living cargo. Depictions of the ark story show a bias in the way we think of animal life. Although most animal species are small invertebrates, artists always show Noah rescuing animals that are big and familiar, such as lions and elephants, rather than worms or insects.

Plants

Plants, like animals, first appeared in water and only later evolved into forms that could cope with conditions on dry land. A plant harnesses the energy in sunlight (p. 14) and uses this energy to turn simple raw materials into food. The simplest plants reproduce sexually by forming microscopic spores, similar to those formed by fungi (p. 51). More advanced plants reproduce by making seeds, which are much more complex packages of cells that usually have a food store and a protective coat. The entire plant kingdom contains over 300,000 species. Representatives of the main groups are shown here.

Spiral wrack

LIVING IN WATER
Seaweeds are multicellular marine algae, simple plant-like organisms that produce spores. Many similar algae live independently as single cells. For this reason, some biologists classify all algae as protists (p. 50) rather than true plants.

FIRST ASHORE
Mosses were among the first plants to live on land. They are non-vascular, having no special channels for carrying water or nutrients, and they have thread-like rhizoids instead of true roots. Most mosses live in damp places, and some live permanently underwater.

ALTERNATING GENERATIONS
Liverworts are simple, often ribbon-like, plants. Like mosses, they have no true roots and they live in damp places. As with all plants, a liverwort's life cycle shows alternation of generations. A stage called a sporophyte, with a double set of chromosomes, alternates with a stage called a gametophyte, which has a single set. Liverworts are unusual in that the gametophyte stage is the dominant stage in the cycle.

Orchid

CARRYING SUPPLIES
Ferns are vascular plants, having special tubes to carry water and nutrients. This allows them to grow much taller than simpler land plants such as mosses and liverworts. Tropical tree-ferns can reach a height of over 20 m (65 ft). Ferns do not have flowers; they reproduce by forming spores.

Male fern

Bishop pine

"MONOCOT" PLANTS
The flowering plants, or angiosperms, number about 250,000 species. They reproduce by seeds but, unlike gymnosperms, their seeds develop inside a protective chamber, or ovary. These plants are divided into two groups. Orchids are typical "monocots" (monocotyledons), having a single seed-leaf, or cotyledon, and parallel-veined leaves.

Larkspur

REPRODUCING WITH SEEDS
Conifers, such as pines, cedars, and redwoods, are "gymnosperms", the first kind of land plants to reproduce by forming seeds rather than spores. Conifer seeds usually form around a hard, woody cone.

DICOT FLOWERING PLANTS
The dicotyledons form the larger of the two groups of flowering plants. Their seeds have two seed-leaves, or cotyledons, their leaves have veins that form a net, and their flower parts are often divided into fours or fives. Like monocots, many of them have evolved elaborate mechanisms for ensuring pollination and seed dispersal. This larkspur has a long tube, or spur, that provides nectar for visiting insects.

Animals

Animals cannot make food by photosynthesis, and they differ from plants in several other ways. All animals can move parts of themselves. Animals respond more quickly to the world around them, and they show patterns of behaviour when they interact with other living things. There are about one million known animal species, classified into some 30 phyla. Some of these phyla contain relatively few species that are found in restricted habitats, such as deep-sea vents. However, the biggest animal phylum – the arthropods (p. 49) – probably contains more species than the other four kingdoms put together.

SIMILAR SEGMENTS
Like all members of the phylum Annelida, an earthworm has a soft body divided into segments. Only the pressure of fluid inside each segment keeps its body in shape. Segmentation is shown by many animal groups, including arthropods and animals with backbones. During the course of evolution, it has often become obscured by later changes in body form.

CNIDARIANS
This hard mineral case was made by a *Fungia* coral. Corals belong to the phylum Cnidaria, which includes sea anemones, *Hydra* (p. 32), and jellyfish. Cnidarians live in water, and catch their food with stinging threads.

MOBILE HOMES
Snails belong to the phylum Mollusca, a large and varied group of animals without backbones. Many molluscs form shells to protect their soft bodies. Not all molluscs are as slow-moving as snails. Cephalopod molluscs, which include squids and octopuses, can move faster than many fish.

ARMOURED CRUST
Crabs are crustaceans, which form the second-largest group of arthropods, after insects. They have a hard body case reinforced with minerals, compound eyes, and several pairs of jointed legs. Like insects, most crustaceans metamorphose, or change body shape, as they grow. Most crustaceans live in water. The woodlouse is one of the few crustaceans to adapt to life on land.

LEADERS IN THE FIELD
This scarab is one of about 800,000 species of insect that have so far been described by biologists. An insect's body is divided into three parts – a head, a thorax that carries the legs and often wings, and an abdomen that contains internal organs. The ability to fly, together with small size, has contributed to the insects' extraordinary success.

Hard plates covering body

THE FIRST VERTEBRATES
Fish were the first animals with backbones to appear on Earth. Today, there are about 20,000 fish species. Most, like this mackerel, have bony skeletons. Sharks, skates, and rays have skeletons made of rubbery cartilage.

FIVE-FOLD SYMMETRY
Starfish belong to the phylum Echinodermata, an unusual group of salt water animals whose bodies are based on the number five. They include sea urchins and sea cucumbers. Their bodies are covered in small, hard plates, and they walk on hundreds of small tube feet.

Rattlesnake

Black-headed starling

Field vole

HALFWAY HOUSE
A frog has a thin, moist skin and spends part of its life in water. It belongs to the class Amphibia, a group of vertebrates that were the first to leave water and venture on to land. Some amphibians live in fairly dry places, but all lay eggs that have to be kept moist. Frogs' eggs produce tadpoles that live in water until they have developed the adult body form.

LIVING ON LAND
Reptiles were the first vertebrates to become fully adapted to life out of water. Unlike amphibians, they lay shelled eggs that retain water, so they can live and breed in dry places. When a young reptile hatches from the egg, it looks like a miniature version of the adult. Reptiles form the class Reptilia. Snakes and lizards make up the largest group of living reptiles.

TAKING TO THE AIR
Birds evolved from reptiles and, like them, they lay shelled eggs. A bird's body is insulated by feathers, and is kept at a high temperature, allowing birds to remain active even in cold surroundings. In order to maintain their temperature and to power their flight muscles, birds need lots of food. Birds make up the class Aves.

MAMMALS
Mammals are warm-blooded animals that have hair and feed their young on milk. They make up the class Mammalia. Most mammals give birth to live young, but the monotremes, which include the duck-billed platypus and two species of spiny anteater, lay eggs. The hair of most land mammals forms a dense coat that keeps the body warm. Many mammals that live in water have lost most of their hair and have a layer of fat, called blubber, to retain their body heat.

How did life begin?

SINCE THE DAWN OF HISTORY, people have wondered how life appeared on our planet. At one time, most people believed that it was specially created. Some still hold this view, but most scientists think otherwise. They believe that the first forms of life were extremely simple, and probably appeared through a series of random chemical reactions nearly 4 million million years ago. Important evidence for this idea came in 1953, when an American chemist called Stanley Miller carried out a crucial experiment. He constructed a sealed chamber that imitated conditions on the early Earth. When he analysed the substances that were produced, he discovered several chemical building blocks that are normally made only by living things. In 1990 another American scientist, Julian Rebek, formed a synthetic chemical that could reproduce itself – a key characteristic of life. Despite these successes, many questions remain about the origins of life. No one knows how simple chemical building blocks came together to form nucleic acids (p. 34), which nucleic acid appeared first, or where life first occurred. Some scientists think that life arose through a rare succession of extremely unlikely events. Others believe that life was almost bound to appear sooner or later.

MYTH AND MAGIC
Before the advent of science, people relied on supernatural events to explain the origin of life. This Mixtec painting from Mexico shows the god Tezcatlipoca and the Earth Monster, from which the Earth was created. Supernatural explanations like this one rely on faith. They cannot be tested by experiments, and they vary between cultures.

LIFE FROM MATTER
The Italian physician Francesco Redi (1626–1697) was one of the first people to test the idea of spontaneous generation, which held that some kinds of life could appear fully formed from non-living matter.

Covered meat

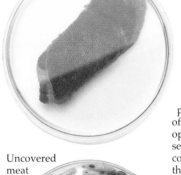

Uncovered meat

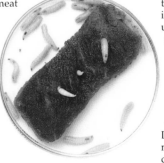

KEEPING LIFE OUT
In the 17th century Francesco Redi tested whether maggots could arise spontaneously from meat, as people then believed. He started by preparing identical pieces of meat. He left some in the open and he put others in sealed flasks or under a covering of gauze. He found that maggots appeared only in the pieces that were left uncovered and accessible to flies. He concluded from this that maggots were always produced by flies and not by the meat itself. In the 18th and 19th centuries, Lazzaro Spallanzani (1729–1799) and the French microbiologist Louis Pasteur showed that not even microorganisms could arise spontaneously.

CRADLE OF THE DEEP
Some of the most ancient forms of life on Earth, the Archaeobacteria (p. 57), live around vents of scalding mineral-laden water deep on the sea bed, obtaining the energy they need by making the minerals react. Deep-sea vents occur across the world's oceans where the plates of the Earth's crust meet. Some scientists think that these vents may have provided the right chemical conditions to act as a cradle for life.

ROOM FOR DOUBT
Not all scientists believe that life started on Earth. The British astronomer Fred Hoyle thinks that the probability of life appearing by accident on Earth is almost zero. He believes life came from space (though this does not explain how life began). Surprisingly complex organic chemicals have indeed been found in space, but the idea of life "seeding" the Earth from space has attracted few supporters.

The spark of life?

In this ground-breaking experiment, Stanley Miller attempted to match atmospheric conditions on Earth about 4 million million years ago. He used an electrical spark to simulate lightning. After running the experiment for a week, he analysed the contents of the flask and found that it contained a number of organic compounds including amino acids, which living things use to make proteins.

Gases and water vapour travel clockwise round apparatus

Clamp

Electrode

Electrode

Spark chamber

STEPS TOWARDS LIFE

In the apparatus that Miller designed, the spark chamber was filled with a mixture of gases, imitating the ancient atmosphere, while the small glass flask, filled with purified water, imitated the primeval sea. Miller simulated lightning by passing an electric discharge between two electrodes in the "atmosphere", and he also heated the "sea". Although it ran for just one week, Miller's experiment produced a variety of organic compounds. In the real world, chemical reactions would have taken place over millions of years, allowing far more complex results. At some point in this long process, chemicals would have appeared that could copy themselves. If this copying process occasionally produced mistakes, which is quite likely, the chemicals would have been able to adapt and evolve by a process called chemical selection. Instead of suddenly appearing, life would have gradually emerged from non-living substances.

Water   Hydrogen

Ammonia

Methane

RAW MATERIALS

In his original experiment, Miller used simple inorganic "ingredients", such as water and ammonia, that he thought would have been present on the early Earth. The energy fed into the apparatus made these substances react to produce a variety of more complex compounds.

Condenser

Urea

THEORY AND TEST

Stanley Miller (above) was the first to test an idea that had been in existence since the 19th century. Charles Darwin speculated about life appearing in a "warm pond". The Russian biochemist Alexandr Oparin (p. 57) was one of the first scientists to speculate about the chemical conditions that may have brought life into being.

Glycine

"FINISHED" PRODUCTS

In the 1950s many scientists were convinced that Stanley Miller's experiment answered the question of how life arose. However, there is a vast gulf in complexity between urea or amino acids, and a much more complex molecule such as deoxyribonucleic acid (DNA). DNA copies itself with the help of enzymes, yet enzymes are themselves made using the information in DNA. This chicken-and-egg situation poses problems that have yet to be answered.

Alanine

Flask of purified boiling water

Source of heat

Complex molecules collect in trap

55

Increasing complexity

TODAY, ALL FORMS OF LIFE ARE MADE UP OF CELLS. These miniature environments are partly sealed from the outside world. They can accumulate substances from the world around them, and can harness energy and reproduce. The Russian chemist Alexandr Oparin was one of the first scientists to study how the earliest cells might have come about. He found that cell-like droplets called coacervates could be made in the laboratory by shaking two complex organic substances together. Later, other chemists discovered that tiny spheres could be formed by warming amino acids. These microspheres have double membranes, just like true cells, and they can also take in raw materials and bud off new microspheres as they grow. As yet, scientists do not know how the first cells actually formed in nature. However, cells have proved to be extremely good at survival, and over millions of years they have evolved different ways of life.

STAYING APART
Oil is insoluble in water. Instead of dissolving, it forms round globules. This happens because oil molecules repel water. They pack together in a round globule because, for a given volume, this shape leaves the fewest molecules in contact with the water. Cell membranes are built of molecules that are partly attracted and partly repelled by water. Instead of forming globules, they form a double layer, just two molecules thick, surrounding a spherical space.

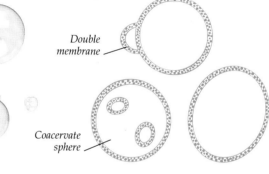

Double membrane

Coacervate sphere

THE LOW-ENERGY BUBBLE
A soap bubble is formed by a thin film of detergent solution. It is round because the solution molecules attract each other, producing a pulling force called surface tension. A spherical shape reduces this tension to a minimum and is most stable. The simplest cells are round for the same reason: a round shape uses least energy.

SPHERES WITHIN SPHERES
A coacervate sphere is a bubble made of tiny globules. It sometimes contains smaller bubbles, mimicking some organelles in a cell. In experiments with coacervate spheres, Alexandr Oparin found that they could use chemical energy to drive simple reactions – a primitive version of metabolism (p. 18). As cells evolved, their metabolism would have gradually become more complex.

Phospholipid molecule

Phospholipid molecule

Protein molecule passing through membrane

Head attracted to water

Tail repelled by water

THE LIQUID MOSAIC
A cell membrane is made up largely of substances called phospholipids. The "head" of each phospholipid molecule is attracted to water, while its "tail" is oily and repelled by it. This polarity makes the molecules line up in a double layer, with their tails facing away from their watery surroundings. According to the fluid-mosaic theory, first proposed in the early 1970s, each layer in the membrane is like a thin sheet of fluid. Instead of being in fixed positions, all its molecules can slide sideways within their layer.

WHICH CAME FIRST?
Alexandr Oparin (1894-1980) thought that cells appeared before genes or proteins. Modern biologists are divided on this issue. Some believe that genes appeared first, while others think that proteins preceded both.

LIVING ON LIGHT (below)
The first living things were chemotrophs, which obtain energy by making chemicals react. Later, cells evolved that could obtain energy by photosynthesis (p. 16). These stromatolites, off the coast of Australia, were gradually built up by cyanobacteria (p. 12), which are among the simplest photosynthetic organisms on Earth.

Iron rusted in presence of oxygen

THE ARRIVAL OF OXYGEN
When life began, there was very little oxygen in the atmosphere. Later, a form of photosynthesis evolved that released oxygen. Although this gas was poisonous to many organisms existing then, oxygen opened up opportunities for living things that were able to make use of it. This atmospheric revolution is recorded in iron-bearing rocks, which rusted as oxygen began to appear.

KINGDOMS AND SUPERKINGDOMS
Living things are often classified in five kingdoms (p. 50), but in the late 1970s a new system was proposed, based on three "superkingdoms". Eukaryotes are organisms whose cells have nuclei, while the two other superkingdoms contain different forms of bacteria, with simpler prokaryotic cells. The more simple bacteria, the Archaeobacteria, probably resemble the first forms of life on Earth.

Mitochondrion from animal cell

Chloroplasts

Chloroplast from plant cell

Eukaryotes; Protists, animals, plants and fungi

MAKING A JUMP
The cells of organisms in the Eukaryote superkingdom contain mitochondria (p. 11) and often have chloroplasts (p. 10). These organelles have a double membrane, contain small amounts of DNA, and can "reproduce" by dividing. They are so similar to some bacteria that many biologists think that they were once free-living organisms.

Mitochondria

Archaeobacteria; Salt-loving bacteria and methane-producing bacteria

Eubacteria; cyanobacteria and mycoplasmas

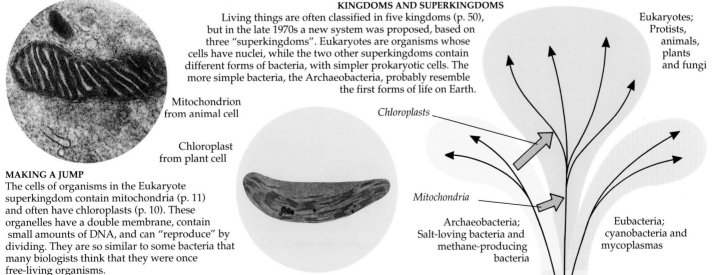

The edge of life

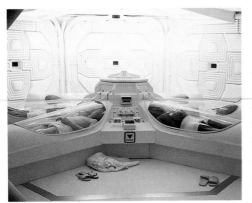

LIFE ON HOLD
In space, a single journey could last years or even decades. In science fiction, space travellers often spend journeys in a deep sleep, so that they do not grow old. One day, this might actually be possible. Many mammals, such as bats and bears, enter a state like this when they hibernate. Their body temperature falls, and their body chemistry slows down. However, unlike viruses, a hibernating mammal still needs energy. Even though it may seem dead to the world, it is still very much alive.

By THE LATE 19TH CENTURY bacteria were known to be agents of disease, or pathogens. They were just large enough to be visible, and the bacteria that caused some diseases had been isolated and identified. However, many diseases remained a puzzle, because their bacteria could not be found. In 1898 the Dutch botanist Martinus Beijerinck (1851-1931) carried out experiments on a disease affecting tobacco plants. He ground up infected plants, and then passed their fluid through a filter fine enough to screen out all known bacteria. He discovered that the filtered fluid was still infectious, so whatever caused the disease had to be even smaller than the smallest bacteria known. Beijerinck called the disease-causing agent a "filterable virus", virus being a Latin word for poison. Scientists now know that viruses are very different from bacteria. Instead of being made of cells, they are tiny packages of chemicals that invade living things. When inside living cells, they behave as if they are alive. Outside living cells, they are completely inert, and they display none of the characteristics of living things.

DRYING UP
Hibernation is just one way of slowing life down. Microscopic tardigrades, or water bears, do the same thing by drying up. These tiny animals live in damp places such as gutters and ditches. If their habitat dries out, they gradually lose most of their body water, and their chemical processes come almost to a standstill. This is called cryptobiosis, or "hidden life". A tardigrade can survive in this state for 50 years or more, and can withstand temperatures as low as −250°C (−418°F).

WAITING TO GROW
Seeds germinate, or sprout, when outside factors, such as moisture or warmth, are suitable for growth. If conditions are not right, they remain dormant. In this state, a seed uses the minimum amount of energy needed to stay alive. These seed-heads are from a lotus. Lotus seeds can germinate after lying dormant for more than a century.

Lotus seed-head

Head containing DNA

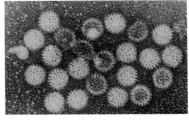

WHEELS OF ILL-FORTUNE
This false-colour electron micrograph shows a collection of rotaviruses, magnified over 70,000 times. These viruses are one of the causes of gastroenteritis in humans, an infection that affects the stomach and intestines. Rotaviruses are named after their wheel-like shape. Each virus has a tough protein coat that protects a molecule of nucleic acid (pp. 34-35).

Tail sheath

LOCKING ON
This is a model of a virus called a T4 bacteriophage. The T4 cannot move about, and it finds a host cell entirely by accident. If it collides with a bacterium, its tail fibres automatically lock on to the bacterium's cell wall and chemical attraction holds it in position. The virus is now ready to inject its DNA into the cell and infect it.

Tail fibre

Tail plate

Plasma membrane of bacterium

Cell wall of bacterium

The world of viruses

The T4 bacteriophage is a virus that copies itself by invading bacteria. Compared with most viruses it is unusually complex, and it has several different parts arranged in a precise way. All viruses contain a strand of nucleic acid (p. 34) that carries the genes needed to assemble new copies of the virus inside a living cell. In the T4 virus the nucleic acid is DNA, but in many other viruses, including the ones that cause AIDS, polio, and the common cold, the nucleic acid is RNA (p. 36). In RNA viruses, "new" RNA is made either by copying "old" RNA directly, or by forming a matching length of DNA first. Biologists are unsure how viruses came about. They may have evolved from single-celled organisms that gradually lost most of their parts. However, they are more likely to be collections of "rogue genes" that have escaped from living cells and evolved a separate existence.

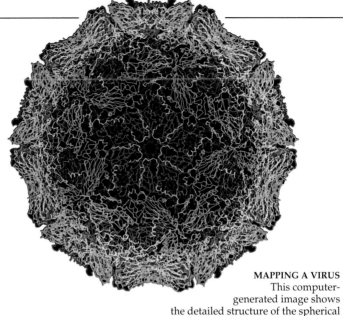

MAPPING A VIRUS
This computer-generated image shows the detailed structure of the spherical protein "coat" surrounding the RNA virus that causes foot and mouth disease in cattle. By using crystallography – the same technique used to investigate DNA (p. 35) – scientists can now pinpoint almost every one of the 300,000 atoms that make up the virus's outer coat. The virus's precise shape allows it to pack together and form crystals.

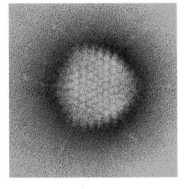

ADENOVIRUS
This electron micrograph shows a single adenovirus, which causes an infection rather like a cold. The virus contains a length of DNA inside a capsid, or protein coat. The capsid has 20 faces, made up of 252 protein units, and at each corner there is a projecting protein spike. These viruses are "naked", which means that they are not surrounded by a membrane, or envelope.

TAKING OVER
Once the T4 bacteriophage has locked on to a bacterium, it produces an enzyme that digests an opening in the bacterium's cell wall. The virus's tail sheath then contracts, and the tail core is pushed through the opening. The virus's DNA travels through the tail core and into the cell, but the rest of the virus stays behind.
It acts as a delivery vehicle and is abandoned once its task is complete. Not all viruses infect their hosts in this way. Some are surrounded by a membrane called an envelope, which links up with the plasma membrane of the host cell, like a small bubble merging with a larger one, and the virus's nucleic acid is drawn into the cell.

A FIVE-STEP HIJACK
A virus makes copies of itself by hijacking the chemical machinery of a living cell. This five-step sequence shows how a T4 bacteriophage carries out the process. The cycle begins with attachment, when the virus locks itself to the cell wall of a bacterium. During the penetration stage the virus's DNA enters the cell. It then takes control of the cell. The cell's normal processes are shut down, and instead it synthesizes many copies of the virus's component parts. In the assembly stage the different parts are brought together to produce new viruses. Finally, the copied, or "replicated", viruses break out of the cell.

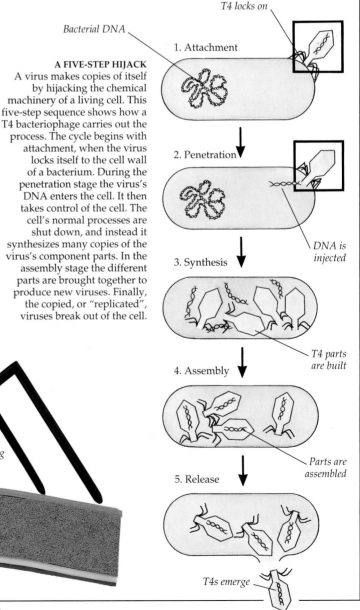

Bacterial DNA

T4 locks on

1. Attachment

2. Penetration

DNA is injected

3. Synthesis

T4 parts are built

4. Assembly

Parts are assembled

5. Release

T4s emerge

Contracted tail sheath

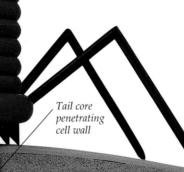

Tail core penetrating cell wall

DNA injected here

Genetic engineering

WHEN A VIRUS INVADES A CELL, something quite remarkable can sometimes happen. Instead of copying itself, the virus's DNA joins up with that of its host and is copied and passed on when its host divides. Many generations later it may suddenly break free to become an independent virus once more. Stranger still, the virus may take some of its host's genes with it, and pass these borrowed genes on when it invades a new cell. This phenomenon, discovered in the 1950s, is called transduction. It shows that genes are interchangeable. Like beads on a necklace, they can swap positions and even jump between DNA strands. In genetic engineering, molecular biologists make use of this facility, slicing up DNA and recombining it so that selected genes are transferred from one organism to another.

JUMPING GENES

In the 1940s the US geneticist Barbara McClintock (1902–1993) made a strange discovery while studying a variety of maize that has multicoloured cobs. She found that the colour variation could only be explained by the existence of moveable pieces of DNA, which are now known as transposons, or "jumping genes". Her work was an early indication that genes may not stay in fixed positions, but at the time it caused little interest. Forty years later, its importance was realized, and Barbara McClintock was awarded a Nobel Prize.

HOW JUMPING GENES WORK

In each of these corn cobs, the kernels are either light or dark. The dark colour is produced by a gene that is present in every cell, but in the cells of some kernels a transposon moves next to the gene and disables it. The result is a light kernel. Transposons have been found in many other organisms, including bacteria and fruit flies. A transposon can duplicate before "jumping", so that many copies build up.

Two identical arms present before cell divides

THE STUFF OF LIFE

These are SEM images of some of the 46 chromosomes found in most human cells. A set of 23 chromosomes contains about 100,000 genes, together with nearly 50 times that amount of "junk" DNA (p. 37). Genes that work together are not always grouped. They may be widely separated on the same length of DNA, or even scattered over several different chromosomes. The entire collection of DNA held by a set of chromosomes has been built up through random change and selection. Our cells contain genes that are useful today as well as others that fell into disuse long ago.

Light kernel

Centromere

Dark kernel

Super-coiled DNA

Human X chromosome

Mutation in gene in this area causes a form of muscular dystrophy

Mutation in gene here causes a disease that affects the eyes

Mutation in gene here causes cleft palate

Mutation in gene here causes haemophilia, a disease that affects blood clotting

Mutation in gene here causes colour blindness

COMPARING DNA

In genetics, the DNA sequence in related organisms often has to be compared. These three strips show just 1/20,000th of the DNA "fingerprint" of three related strains of bacteria. In each strip, four columns show the occurrence of each of the four bases – guanine (G), adenine (A), thymine (T), and cytosine (C) (p. 34). The three strains are almost identical, but there is one difference in the bases between strain 1 and strain 2, and four differences between strains 2 and 3. This tells the geneticist that 1 and 2 diverged from each other more recently than they diverged from 3. This kind of sequence print is produced by a process called electrophoresis, in which an electric field causes DNA to move through a thin gel. Such prints can be used to identify individuals, because everybody – except identical twins – has a unique DNA sequence.

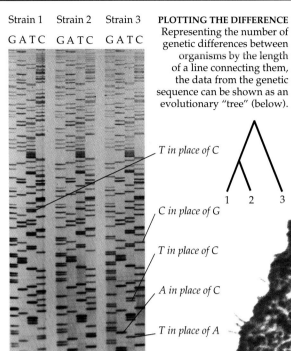

Strain 1 Strain 2 Strain 3
G A T C   G A T C   G A T C

T in place of C

C in place of G

T in place of C

A in place of C

T in place of A

PLOTTING THE DIFFERENCE

Representing the number of genetic differences between organisms by the length of a line connecting them, the data from the genetic sequence can be shown as an evolutionary "tree" (below).

1 2 3

MAPPING A CHROMOSOME

In the Human Genome Project, teams of scientists are currently trying to establish the exact position of every gene carried on human chromosomes. When this massive undertaking is complete, it will enable genetic engineers to target disabling genes and perhaps inactivate or replace them. This outline map (above) shows the areas in which a few of the genes carried on the human X chromosome are found. Each one is present as two copies, with one on each of the chromosome's opposing arms, or chromatids.

THE GENETIC DATABASE

The entire human genome contains about 3 billion base-pairs. Without computers, charting and analysing this vast amount of chemical information would be almost impossible. This computer screen shows a small part of a base-pair sequence. Geneticists can scan parts of the genome for particular sequences that indicate the start or end of a gene.

PUTTING GENES TO WORK

Genetic engineering, or recombinant DNA technology, has many practical applications. This field contains crop plants that have been genetically engineered to withstand the effects of a herbicide that is used to kill weeds. Genetic engineers can also transfer resistance to disease from one organism to another. In medicine, one of the most valuable achievements of genetic engineers has been to make bacteria produce human insulin. Insulin is needed by people with diabetes, and previously it came from animals.

5 The protein produced by the gene may be collected and used.

5 Copies of the gene may be collected, so that they can be inserted into another organism.

MAKING GENES MOVE

At present, genetic engineering is mainly carried out by inserting genes into bacteria. A gene is first identified, and then sliced out of its DNA strand by special proteins called restriction enzymes. Each one works like a pair of chemical scissors, cutting the DNA at a particular sequence of bases. The gene is then combined with a plasmid, a small circular piece of DNA found in a bacterium. When the bacterium divides, the plasmid is copied and handed on. The result is millions of bacteria that all contain the new gene. The gene, or the protein that it produces, can then be harvested.

1 The gene is identified and located. This gene is in a bacterial chromosome.

2 The DNA is sliced up by a restriction enzyme. Each piece has two "sticky ends" that can join up with other DNA.

3 A bacterial plasmid is sliced open and the length of DNA containing gene is inserted.

4 The plasmid is reintroduced into a bacterium. When the bacterium divides, the plasmid is copied and passed on.

Life beyond Earth?

THE EARTH IS JUST ONE PLANET AMONG MANY, and our Sun is just one star among billions in the Universe as a whole. To some scientists, these facts suggest that life may well exist elsewhere but, despite countless reports of UFOs and visits by aliens, no direct evidence of extraterrestrial life has ever been found. Scientists must therefore rely on guesswork to explore the possibility of life elsewhere. One of the first to apply mathematics to this guesswork was the American scientist Frank Drake. The Drake Equation estimates the number of advanced civilizations in our galaxy alone by multiplying seven factors, including the number of stars in our galaxy, the proportion that have planets, and the proportion of planets on which life may have appeared. Unfortunately, most of these factors are very difficult to estimate. Some values give the number of advanced civilizations as zero, while with others it runs into millions.

BARREN NEIGHBOUR
All life on Earth is based on water. Water has some remarkable properties: it is a very good solvent, its molecules cling together very tightly, and instead of contracting when it freezes, it expands. The Moon is totally lacking in water, and this is one of the reasons why it is also lacking in life.

THE WAR THAT WASN'T
In his famous science fiction novel *The War of the Worlds*, H.G. Wells (1866-1946) described an imaginary invasion of the Earth by beings from Mars. In 1938, when the story was broadcast by radio in the US, many people fled from their homes in panic.

LOST IN TRANSLATION
In 1877 the Italian astronomer Giovanni Schiaparelli (1835-1910) drew these maps of the surface of Mars. They feature long streaks that he thought were filled with water. He called these *canali*, meaning channels. When the word was translated into English as "canals", people thought that Martians had dug them.

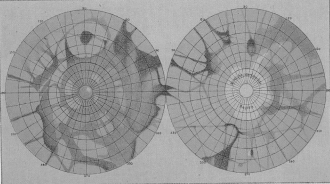

LIFE IN THE MAKING
The view below shows an imaginary scene on a distant planet, bathed by the light and warmth of two Suns. Jostled by this supply of energy, chemicals in the atmosphere and water would join in the endless round of reactions that might one day produce the building blocks of life. Whether this life would look anything like living things on Earth, we can only guess. The evolution of life is full of unexpected successes, catastrophic failures, and gradual dead ends. No one can predict its outcome.

MORE ON MARS

Fired by Schiaparelli's discovery of "canals" on Mars, the American astronomer Percival Lowell (1855-1916) drew his own detailed maps showing criss-crossing waterways. His work convinced many people that Mars was inhabited, but he was probably influenced by his enthusiasm for the idea of Martian life. When space probes passed close to Mars in the 1960s, no canals were seen, and two Viking probes that carried out experiments on the surface of the planet in the 1970s failed to detect any signs of life.

GETTING IN TOUCH

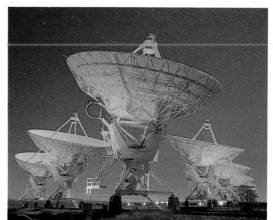

If there is life elsewhere in the Universe, it is likely to be immensely distant. Since the 1970s, various messages in the form of radio signals have been beamed into space in the hope of making contact. However, even a radio wave would take four years to reach the nearest star, so many centuries may pass before our calls are answered.

SCIENCE FACT OR SCIENCE FICTION?

In science fiction it is taken for granted that space travel will soon be common, but history may show this to be wrong. The Earth's human population is increasing at a dramatic rate, and millions of people already lack the basic resources that they need for daily life. Simple economics mean that we may never manage to spread beyond our planet.

ISLANDS IN SPACE

Our galaxy contains about 100 billion stars, arranged in a spiral disc that is slowly rotating in space. The Andromeda galaxy, shown here, is one of our closest galactic neighbours, and it probably contains twice as many stars as our own. Astronomers have discovered that planetary systems are probably quite common, so in any one galaxy millions of stars may be orbited by worlds that are suitable for life.

Index

Acknowledgments

Dorling Kindersley would like to thank:

Nigel Cope of A. J. Cope and Son Ltd for advice and provision of laboratory equipment; Gerald Legg at the Booth Museum of Natural History, Brighton, for the provision of objects for photography; Paul Field of Fur, Feathers 'n' Fins, Lewes, for provision of animals for photography; Jill Carpenter and Noel Smith of the University of Sussex for the DNA sequence and advice; Terry Tribe of Chemglassware for special laboratory equipment; Wellcome Museum of Anatomy at the Royal College of Surgeons for special photography; Martin Stenning of the University of Sussex for technical advice; Simonne Dearing, Dingus Hussey and Sarah Brigham for design assistance; Sharon Jacobs for proofreading; Stephen Bull and Alan Jackson for illustrations; Jane Burton, Peter Chadwick, Andy Crawford, Geoff Dann, Richard Davies, Mike Dunning, Andreas von Einsiedel, Philip Gatward, Steve Gorton, Frank Greenaway, Dave King, Cyril Laubscher, Bill Ling, Tim Ridley, Science Museum, Science Museum Library, Tim Shepard, Harry Taylor, Kim Taylor, and Jerry Young for additional photography.

Model on page 15 supplied by Somso Modelle, Coburg, Germany.

Illustrations John Woodcock
Model-making Wendy Chandler and Ian Whitelaw
Index Jane Parker

Publisher's note No animal has been injured or in any way harmed during the preparation of this book.

Picture credits

t=top b=bottom c=centre l=left r=right

Allsport/Mike Powell: 19bc. Bodleian Library, Oxford: 48c. Boehringer Ingelheim International /Gmbh/Lennart Nilsson: 28c. Bridgeman Art Library: 7t Ny Carlsberg Glyptothek. David Burnie: 23tl. Bruce Coleman Ltd: /R. Carr 19c /Jeff Foott 39tr /Micheal Glover 21cl /Hans Reinhard 31br /Frieder Sauer 21tr. Mary Evans Picture Library: 8bl, 9tl, 12bl, 15t, 16tr, 18cl, 19cr, 20tl, 23c, 25c, 25tl, 26cr, 29bl, 29br, 32bl, 37cr, 40tl, 43c, 48tl, 50tl, 52tl, 62cl, 62cr. Werner Forman Archive: 54tl Liverpool Museum. Greenpeace/Dorréboom: 20cl. Dr Gary Grimes: 46-7. Derek Hall: 47tl, 47cr. Hoechst A. G: 27br /Image Bank: 26cl, 36tr. Kobal: 63cl. Life Science Images: 25bl. Oxford Scientific Films /Phil Devries: 33br. Planet Earth Pictures: /Gary Bell 39cr /Colin Doeg 47cl. Press Association: 54br. Science Photo Library: 9tr, 10cl, 14tl, 35cr, 55cl, 58cr, 63tl /Jeremy Burgess 12tl /Dr L. Caro 50bl /Dr R. Clark & M. R. Goff 18c /Daudier, Jerrican 6tl /Tony Hallas 63cr /Manfred Kage 32cr, 50c /Peter Menzel 17cl, 61bl /Sidney Moulds 51bl /Dr Gopal Murti 34br /NASA 62tl /National Library of Medicine 38tl /Novosti 57tl /Oxford Molecular Biophysics Lab. 59t /Photoresearches 35tl /Philippe Plailly 61c /John Reader 57c /Roger Ressmeyer, Starlight 63tr /Robert Schuster 58cl /Peter Ryan Scripps 54c /Chris Taylor, CSIRO 15bl /M. Wurtz, Biozentrum, University of Basel 59c. Suddeutscher Verlag 45bl. UPI/Bettmann Archive 60tl. Trustees of the Wellcome Institute: 16bl, 54cl.